The Not-So-Helpless Female

The Not-So

How to Change the World Even if You Never Thought You Could
A Step-by-Step Guide to Social Action

by Tish Sommers

Helpless Female

lrawings by Genny Güracar (Bülbül)

AVID McKAY COMPANY, INC. / NEW YORK

The Not-So-Helpless Female

LIBRARY OF CONGRESS CATALOG CARD NUMBERS: 72-86968

MANUFACTURED IN THE UNITED STATES OF AMERICA

DESIGNED BY JACQUES CHAZAUD

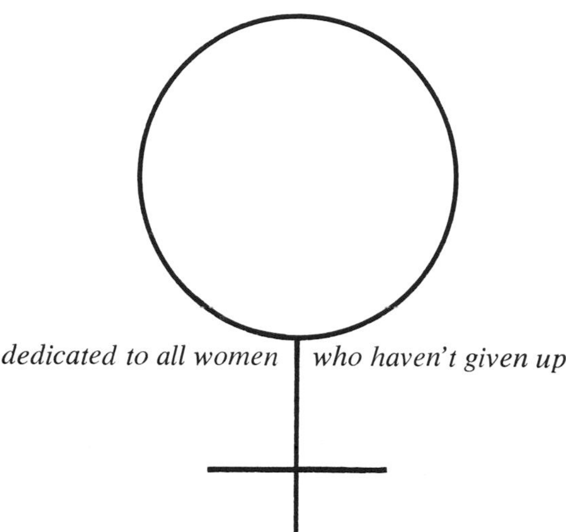
dedicated to all women who haven't given up

Contents

Introduction: The New Spirit of Activism xi

PART I

Self-Organization

Start with Number One

1. That Flabby Ego 4
2. Guilt and the Pedestal 9
   Things to Feel Guilty About—Mom the Flak-Catcher—But Isn't Guilt What Really Gets You Going?—Consciousness-Raising
3. Breaking Out of the Cage 13
   One Dozen Cage-Breakers
4. Self-Organization 16
   Suburban Glossary—Tips for Getting It Together—A Gallery of Put-It-Offs
5. Starting Points 22
   Housewives' Handicap System for Ego-Building—What-Is-My-Thing Inventory for Getting Started
6. Push-ups to Get Started 25
   Examples of Push-ups—Escalating a Push-up
7. Write On! 30
   Comments from the Receiving End—To Whom?—

Types of Letters—Carbon Copy—Sample Letter—Sample Cover Letter—Escalating a Letter

8. Volunteer Beware! 37
Suburban Glossary—Volunteer Traps—Valid Volunteering—V.V. Test (for Valid Volunteerism)

9. New Careers for Volunteers 44
Career Ladders Out of Volunteerism

10. Volunteer Power 50
Take the Pledge—Sample Letter—Do Something . . . for Change

11. Vocations and Careers for Social Change 54

12. Become an Expert 57
How to Go About Becoming an Expert

13. What One Turned-On Person Can Do 61

PART II

Working in Groups

14. Banding Together 68
The Long Road to Action—Strike a Balance—We Band Together for Power—Criteria for Selecting an Organization—Or, Form Your Own—The Question of Style—Blasting Off

15. Finding Teammates 82
Teaming Techniques—How to Hold a Public Meeting—Our Woman in City Hall (Cultivating the Grass Roots)

16. The Caucus 91

17. Meetings and Their Hang-Ups 93
Meeting Analysis—One Dozen Cage-Breakers for Meetings—Criteria for Determining Where Any Group Is At

18. Strategy and Tactics 101
Choosing the Issue—Necessary Homework

19. Planning the Strategy 110
The Ideological Peg—Sample Strategy

20. The Crisis Theory of Social Action 115
When the Crisis Comes, Move Out with the Action

21. Tactics 119
Alinsky's Rules for Tactics Feminized—Tactics for the New Woman

22. Co-opt the System 126
Law 'n' Order—Sue 'Em!—Co-opter's Glossary

23. Mass Media: The Beloved Monster 138
What's News?—Orchestrate the News—Madison Avenue on Our Side?—Meet the Press—Radio Is Not Dead—We *Can* Talk Back to Our Televisions—Media of Our Very Own

24. The Queen's English, or Linguistic Activism 148
If You've Got a Lemon, Make Lemonade

25. Role Your Own 152
Brainstorming—Rehearsals—Games People Should Play—Zaps—Guerrilla Theater—Props and Costumes —Visual Aids

26. Money (I): Its Dangers and How to Get It 164
Fund Raising as the Pros Do It—Thirty-five Ways to Raise Money—Putting It On

27. Money (II): Grantswomanship 176
Financial Actions

28. Toward a Positive New Woman's Style 181
Some Elements of the New Style

PART III

Alliances—Coalitions—Conferences

29. Finding Common Ground 188

30. Joint Action 189

31. Coalitions 195
Significant Models—Coalition Politics—Problems of Coalition—One Dozen Coalition-Builders

32. The Conference 209
A Conference Budget
A Conference Checklist

PART IV

Creating the Phoenix While Rome Burns

33. Why Do We Keep Trying to Build While the Flames Roar? 218
The Phoenix Redefined—The Major Pitfalls

34. Where Will It All Lead? 227

35. Freedom and Responsibility: A Feminist View 231

Notes and Sources 235

Introduction: The New Spirit of Activism

This is a book on doing something about those things we feel are wrong. Generations of the passive role have taken a toll, so that many of us feel more helpless than we really are. For too long we've been expected to watch and applaud (or lament, as the case may be). Or busy ourselves with trivia in the name of a social cause. Well, good riddance to all that, because neither we nor our planet can afford such a waste of time.

There is a changing mood among women, a decided shift of gears, which presages a new spirit of activism. While this has only begun, the effects have been remarkable when compared with past performance. When measured against the tasks that society faces, the results seem minuscule, which too often leads to discouragement. At this stage we need a great deal of help from each other, plenty of support, and the sharing of those techniques that work. This guide to action is for that purpose.

Like all books, it reflects the authors' premises. These are ours: We are feminists. By that we mean that we have a growing and changing philosophy that includes acceptance of ourselves as women, a liking for others of our sex, and a sense of direction based upon the first two. We believe that feminism includes taking responsibility for onself, which in turn implies a shared responsibility for others and for the world. At the core of all that is one's own personhood.

Second, we conceive of all issues as women's issues (and, in turn, of women's issues as everyone's province). There was a time when our concerns could be segregated, but no more. This doesn't imply that we should be pulled aside from working for our own interests. On the contrary: only by fighting our own battles can we really have impact as social movers. But a female activist who stops a polluter is making as great a breakthrough for her sex as the woman whose job requires her to climb a telephone poll, whatever either of them has to say about "Women's Lib."

Third, we anticipate no conflict between humanism and feminism. The major problems of the day belong to all of us whether we like it or not, and most of them overlap. As world-changers we may travel down separate paths, but it is the direction in which we are going that matters. In any case, we can't travel very far with others on our backs. Or riding on someone else's back.

Fourth, we see social change as essential to survival—at least, those changes that straighten out our distorted values. And because survival is at stake, we feel hope, not despair. We think we're going to make it.

The first part of the book is about breaking out of old patterns. Retooling can't be done all at once, but is a continuous process. The second part deals with working in groups, both from the inside and moving outward to alter "the system" (those institutions that perpetuate the old). The third part extends group action to alliances and coalitions, the development of "our side" in a larger sense. Last, there is a look at activism and some of its pitfalls from a feminist viewpoint.

We hope this book will move things along. It is based on the work and experience and the ideas of a lot of us who realize that we're all in this together, learning from each other.

—Tish Sommers
—Genny Güracar (Bülbül)

The Not-So-Helpless Female

Note: For information on how to contact groups mentioned, see Note and Sources, p. 235.

Self-Organization

Start with Number One

EGO

1.
THAT FLABBY EGO

How many women's meetings have you attended this year? Did they accomplish much? Probably not, if they were like the familiar scene that follows:

A group of ladies is sitting in a comfortable clubroom. The purpose of their meeting is to discuss what the group might do about welfare (or pollution, open spaces, race relations, the plight of the Indian, or ending war). These are intelligent women; most have some college education. They are the "concerned" elite of any church, neighborhood, or women's organization. The meeting may go something like this:

MRS. ANDREWS: (chairing) Well, we've heard speakers on this problem for six sessions now. Some of us feel we really should *do* something. What *can* we do?

MRS. BAKER: Mr. Hall said we should get a petition going.

MRS. COLLINS: Do we really know that much about it? Perhaps we should first conduct a survey among all our members and see how they feel. What do you think, Prudence?

MRS. ANDREWS: I'm not too sure . . . How long would it take to make a survey?

MRS. DOBBS: Maybe we could plan a program for the annual spring luncheon.

MRS. EDWARDS: I don't think the executive board would be too happy about that. They've been talking about Japanese floral arrangements for the theme this year.

MRS. ANDREWS: (two hours and no decision later) Since

many of us have to leave to be home when school is out, perhaps we should refer these suggestions to the executive board. Let's all give Mrs. Fisher a round of applause for her delicious refreshments. . . .

Is this meeting a success or a failure? Both. Nothing, except due mention in the annual report of "accomplishments," will happen in regard to the issue discussed, but as a ritual it is quite satisfying. It helps allay the uneasiness caused by the earlier speakers, who presented the worrisome problem. Most of the participants share a sense of commitment to a social concern and the good feeling of having "done what we could." Nobody is upset.

If the daughter of one of those women were visiting, however, she would probably want to run out shrieking, "Impossibly dull! What did they accomplish? Liberation!"

Let's analyze the meeting, looking for what it reveals about women who take part in this recurrent ritual:

§ *"What can we do?"* These women have weak egos, especially when venturing outside their own domain. The problems seem so immense, and they are just little people.

§ *"Mr. Hall said . . ."* They are accustomed to being followers, not initiators.

§ *"We don't know that much . . ."* Suppose they are wrong—it might cause controversy.

§ *"I'm not too sure . . ."* Assertiveness is to be avoided at all costs. Leaders are subject to criticism.

§ *"I don't think the executive board . . ."* Women are more often harmonizers than fighters.

§ ". . . *have to leave to be home* . . ." The real world is calling.

§ ". . . *perhaps we should refer* . . ." Everything is left in good order, the way it's supposed to be.

The daughter who might have left shrieking would consider herself at the opposite pole. Her group is more likely to be discussing "woman" issues:

DEBBIE: (just begins; no one chairs) Women are short-changed in so many ways. When you go to a doctor, he never tells you anything.

SHERRIE: Like, we should have a woman's clinic.

LORI: That could be just a big ego trip for somebody.
ROZ: How do we know people would use it? Maybe we ought to put up a notice in the laundromat and see what people say.
KERRI: Let me tell you what happened to me once . . .
DEBBIE: (two hours and no decision later) Some of us have to leave now, so let's take this up at the big meeting next week.

This has not yet hardened into a ritual; anything could happen, but the sins of the mothers are reappearing:

§ *"We should have . . ."* A promising start.

§ *"Could be just a big ego trip for somebody." Lack* of ego is what is holding back the trip for everybody.

§ *"How do we know?"* There is never certainty or enough information.

§ *"Let me tell you . . ."* The comfortable evasion of a hard problem.

§ *"Let's take this up at the big meeting."* The decision is off their backs for a while at least.

Doesn't it seem a contradiction? Women probably are more disposed to work for community good than most men; genetic differences aside, it's part of our nurturing, peacemaker, humanistic upbringing. Yet those very qualities that have made women concerned human beings have been turned to our disadvantage, much as judo turns an attacker's strength back against him. The effect is negative in two ways: women are caught in self-defeating trivialities, and society is deprived of vital contributions that we could make.

On the one hand, most of us have weak egos. On the other, we are imbued with an ideal of saintliness that adds to the strain. This may not be immediately apparent in the barrage of piggish images the media project, but selflessness as a code for women to live by is so much a part of our experience that it goes unquestioned. We are no more conscious of it than fish are aware that water is wet. Take a look at the advice offered in some recent books of advice to women:

> . . . you will have learned to give more than your share, how to help him through trying times, how to rejoice in his triumph. . . . Certainly your husband need never thank you for

> helping him through college. Perhaps you should thank *him* for giving you the chance of this experience. . . .
>
> . . . The dedicated seldom have a personal goal. Fulfillment comes to them through the knowledge that others have been or are being or will be benefited by their services. . . . It has been observed that almost without exception behind every outstanding executive a dedicated secretary selflessly functions.
>
> . . . Being a volunteer only requires a frame of mind—the desire to do something, with no financial reward, for someone else who could not receive that service unless *you* do it with him or for him.

This incredibly high moral plane on which we are supposed to function is so unrealistic that it generates a heavy load of guilt. It also makes us fearful of upsetting anyone and ashamed of involving ourselves in a cause in our own interests. It makes us try to appear innocuous and self-abasing. Traditional feminine rewards are internal ones: a clear conscience, a sense of satisfaction, and reassurance of essential goodness. Masculine rewards are generally external: money, status, recognition, and power.

The question is not how to replace feminine rewards with masculine ones, or to substitute so-called male values for female ones. The trick is to find a better balance—a more equitable sharing of rewards and responsibilities. Especially it is to learn how woman's strengths can be brought to bear upon society's ills, not turned back on herself.

GUILT
YE OLD
PEDESTAL

2.
GUILT AND THE PEDESTAL

A woman soliciting for one of the dread diseases came to the door one day. While making a small donation, I said something positive about her coming by. This prompted a sad tale of how she didn't really want to be doing it. She had told the agency so, but they promised "Just this time, and only a small territory." About a month later she was back at the door, collecting in the name of another disease. Same complaints. "Never again," she said. Considering her position a month ago, I asked why she had accepted. "I just didn't see how to refuse. I would have felt guilty."

That wasn't volunteer work; that was involuntary servitude, even though the jailer was in her own head.

Things to Feel Guilty About

Take a paper and pencil and make a list of all the things you feel guilty about. Here are some common ones:

Too much community work and neglecting the family; not fulfilling my quota; no time for the church; spending so much time there that my children feel like orphans; not supportive enough of my husband's interests; taking over too much for him; insensitive to the neighbor with the problem; being a doormat, always available; not visiting people who are handicapped or sick; always doing for others and neglecting my own; letting my figure spread; too concerned about appearance; spending hard-earned money; tight-pursed; wasting time shopping; missing the best bargains; becoming a pack rat; throwing useful things out; being a worrying mom; not keeping an eye on the kids; too permissive; too strict; the children aren't developing independence; neglecting them; using the wrong color toilet paper; wasting water while washing dishes; not making my own clothes; always sewing; putting the children in a childcare center to go back to school; being a stick-in-the-mud housewife; wasting time reading the papers; not keeping up with the world; polluting the air with leaded gasoline; worrying about what the new gas is doing to our car; driving the kids too much; not taking them where they want to go; holding the children too close to home; worrying about where they are; giving the children too many things; depriving them of advantages other children have; letting them watch too much TV; not having a TV set in the house . . .

Stop writing! A treadmill of guilt will get you nowhere.

Mom the Flak-Catcher

It's human to find someone else to blame, preferably a victim who's not organized and can't fight back. Who fits the bill in our society? *Mom.* If schools are under attack, it is more convenient to talk about parents (translate "mother") than to confront school personnel or methods. If a man is injured in the rough-and-tumble of cut-throat competition, it's not the hassle to blame: it's his penis-envying mother. The black woman receives a double dose of blame, particularly from former presidential adviser Patrick Moynihan. As he sees it, the matriarchal family with its overly dominant woman is the root of ghetto problems, not discrimination in jobs or housing. Since expulsion from Eden, there are few problems that someone has not blamed on woman.

The answer to all this is to say "none of that for me" when a new reason to feel guilty is offered. Unfortunately, we are all too well-conditioned to add to an already heavy burden. So, for our sanity and freedom to function, we must learn to push back.

Avoid adding new guilts to the old. A woman newly concerned for the environment who replaces paper napkins with cloth, without eliminating other tasks or attacking the problem beyond her personal responsibility, may feel worse than ever. One who says, "My life has been too selfish; I really want to be involved with other people," and thus adds a collection of dependent persons to her accumulation of things, may just collapse under it all. What we don't need is to recycle old guilt.

But Isn't Guilt What Really Gets You Going?

"Should" is a much over-rated fuel for goading a person into action. It is supposed to galvanize you, but generally it stops you in your tracks. Concern is something else—including concern for oneself. Guilt slows us down; concern moves us out. Guilt is self-directed (I did wrong; I'm not okay); concern is other-directed (This is my interest; I'm okay). When we are feeling guilty, we are comparing ourselves with an ideal of conduct that may be a myth, an unrealistic version of a female on a pedestal that we inherited from our grandmothers. It's past time to climb off that pedestal and meet each other.

Consciousness-Raising

As we begin to change things, we change, too. Somewhere along the way comes the need to understand what is happening inside our heads. At this point, we will most likely be looking for others who feel the same way.

The Women's Liberation Movement calls this process "consciousness-raising," and has developed autonomous small groups to fill the need. Here is the way one such collective looks at it:

> We have defined our group as a place in which to think: to think about our lives, our society and our potential for being creative individuals and for building a woman's movement. We call this Free Space. We have successes and failures in utilizing this space. . . . Individual integrity—intellectual and emotional honesty—is our goal. It has been and is a difficult struggle. . . .
>
> We have developed four group processes to help us in our endeavors to become autonomous in our thinking and behavior. We call these processes opening up, sharing, analyzing and abstracting.

My own experience with consciousness-raising groups—the "small groups" of the Women's Liberation Movement—has been good. By opening up and sharing, I feel the warm trust and emotional support for the lonely task of redefining myself. Analyzing and abstracting—much harder to do, and not always realized—is a very creative experience. When it happens in a collective * situation, sisterhood is no longer a word but a state of mind. Small groups cannot bridge all gaps in communication and problem sharing. Many experience a split between personal support and action. "We get so personal that we lose sight of the universal We're awfully entrenched in the history of our lives," said one member. Another said, "Rapping alone provides no outlet for the anger felt by women."

One activist felt that she was in a small group primarily for support. "My consciousness is already raised beyond my ability to put my understanding into practice. Women need the supportive aspects of the small group, but it is only through putting energy into change that one can relieve the frustration that grows out of consciousness-raising."

The weaknesses of the small groups are also their strengths. By moving from personal to common problems, women learn to talk to each other as human beings, to cope with fear, to view problems not just abstractly but in living terms. The small group form has given depth to the woman's movement.

New small groups are constantly forming with the assistance of veterans. Women's centers and bookstores can provide the names of coordinators. When contacted, an established small group schedules an orientation session and helps the new members get themselves together. Some organize an evening's discussion around a topic, such as "growing older female"; some agree to discuss a book or article that everyone has read. They learn by trial and error the forms that are most productive for their own members.

The idea of consciousness-raising can be extended to other movements beyond women's liberation. Whites engaged in the struggle against racism find the need for probing their unconscious attitudes before they can effectively move against them. Coping with hostility comes to the fore with pacifists. Before too long,

* "Collective" is used as an adjective, to describe a way of working together cooperatively, not competitively, with trust, honesty, and sharing. As a noun, it refers to a group that is structured and working collectively (or at least attempting to).

ecologists will be asking each other how their theories will affect their own values and lifestyles.

It's especially good for women to get together and talk about these things. Consciousness is defined as inward sensibility, knowledge of one's own existence, the collective thoughts and feelings of an individual. That's a lot to do, and in reaching for it we can use a little help from each other.

3.
BREAKING OUT OF THE CAGE

Consider the well-known prayer of Alcoholics Anonymous:

> God grant me the serenity to accept the things I cannot change . . .
> The courage to change the things I can change . . .
> And the wisdom to know the difference.

Most of us are quite strong on point one; we have been well-trained for that. Away from home, we're weak on point two, and we haven't had enough experience to do well with the third. We're still inside a cage of feminine mystification. To gain that wisdom for point three, each of us will have to break out of her cage, whether it be rusty or gilded, a decorator's dream or a conventional split-level.

One Dozen Cage-Breakers

(1) *Give a karate yell.* The new enthusiasm for self-defense classes for women is based on more than the practical value of repulsing an attacker. A young women who teaches such a class states, "When a woman takes self-defense she soon shunts off her child status and isn't afraid to criticize what's wrong in her environment. This is the first step to constructive change, so it is

good for everyone." In private, stand in the classic karate position —feet slightly apart, knees bent for balance—then pull the elbows in sharply to the ribs an exhale with an explosive *haaaaaaaa!* The cage will tremble.

(2) *Set priorities.* Others may think your time is expendable. You can't. Make up a list, something like this:

A. My Number-One Priority (On this I will not be moved!): *Do not disturb.*
B. These cannot be avoided—unfortunately.
C. These I will try to get to:

(a) Must do something about this—it's been waiting to become number one. (b) Not too sure about these. Must make up my mind. (c) Perhaps can be delegated—to whom? (d) May have to scrap.

(3) *Call a friendly family council.*

MOTHER: Look, darlings, you know how bad water pollution is and how concerned I am about the future. Well, I've started on this project . . .

SON: We're proud of you, Mom. Can we do anything to help?

DAUGHTER: I'll pitch in with the housework.

FATHER: We'll *all* pitch in. It's everybody's house, isn't it? And if your mother is working for cleaner water for all of us . . .

ALL (cries in chorus): We're a great family! Right on, Mom!

It doesn't go like that in your house? Well, there's something to work toward.

(4) *Set deadlines.* Every housewife knows how quickly the closets are cleaned when her mother-in-law is coming to visit. Housework increases to fill the time available, and so does "social action" busywork. So, plan in an equivalent of a mother-in-law visit on any project.

(5) *Find the folks with kindest strokes.* The bleaker things look, the more you need the gentle touch of friends' encouragement. Seek out the ones you know will be supportive, not the doomsayers. Honest support, though, not flattery.

(6) *Write ten times: "I am an adult."* We females dearly want it both ways: safe and rewarding. Protection and constant reassurance are for children. Adults get battered over and over. Each

time we are hurt, we would like to go back to little-girl habits and decide that nothing is possibly worth the struggle.

(7) *Prepare a first-aid box for self-pity.* Sample items: profanities of your choice (very useful to counteract the baby tears); worse-off model for comparison (such as "How would I like to be fighting for my dignity and self-fulfillment in Pakistan?"); objective viewer (such as "This should give me new insight into similar situations. Very valuable evidence."); sister in need of help (advice or assistance offered does much to pick up the spirits of the giver).

(8) *One-year plan for downward social mobility.* If too much is your problem, rather than too little, begin to move away from middle-class consumerism to a simpler, more human lifestyle. Fewer accessories means less dusting. Try a pact with a friend not to go inside a store (except for groceries) for one week (or month). Shop selectively, according to your interests (avoid war manufacturers, polluters, etc.).

(9) *Prepare in advance comebacks for comments you abhor.*

COMMENT: You housewives have it good. You don't know how lucky you are.

ANSWER: The average housewife works a 99.6-hour work week. At going rates she would receive $257 per week—if paid—according to figures compiled by the Chase Manhattan Bank.

COMMENT: Why do you interest yourself in that? Politics is too dirty for a woman.

ANSWER: Not as dirty as housework.

(10) *Reinforce the positive.* Where and when do you get your best ideas? In the shower? Garden? Early? Late? While cooking? Are you a "lark" or an "owl"? Work with your own physiological rhythm.

(11) *Fail at something.* Fear of failing is a strong deterrent. Experience the good feeling of knowing that you can pick yourself up and move on. The soundest learning comes through failure.

(12) *"I can"* is the best cage-breaker of all. Tattoo it on your soul.

4.
SELF-ORGANIZATION

Suburban Glossary

"I just can't find the time." I don't have a schedule because other people decide my time for me.

"I'm not well-enough informed to have an opinion on that." I don't read the paper except for the recipes, because I'm not expected to make decisions.

"I never can find anything." This is just busywork anyway.

Tips for Getting It Together

Time

Use your best hours for skull work, less favorable ones for housework. If there are small children, never do domestic work when they nap. Do the *real* (world-changing) work first, chores later. Set priorities. A daily list, setting off the "must do" from the "should do," helps from getting snowed.

Place

Set aside a place. It can be a desk or a corner, but not the kitchen table. When a woman begins to take herself seriously, she usually starts a filing system. A miscellaneous pile of papers reflects hopelessness and self-contempt. A file can be made by covering a liquor box or liberating a file drawer.

WARNING: It's fine to provide a friend with information on upcoming legislation or locate a year-old letter, but if filing becomes an end in itself, it has defeated its purpose. You have become bureaucratized. It's a good idea to weed out inactive files and store them. A small working file kept up to date is worth the effort.

Information

Television is good for getting a general overview. Watching a daily newsprogram helps to keep a check on major news currents, and the visual impact reinforces other media.

Radio is useful because you can listen to the news while engaged in other activities, like driving or housework.

Newspapers are necessary for local coverage and for clipping.

Newsletters and fact sheets are especially valuable for legislative information and specialized coverage of activities in a particular field.

Magazines can be scanned at the supermarket. As more women become activists, even traditional female journals are carrying substantive articles. An occasional check through the periodicals section of the library (can be done with the children) usually pays off.

Clipping

This can be a time-consuming task and a dead end, or it can be a helpful step toward accomplishing something further. Clippings are useful for developing a file of specifics on your favorite concern, preparing an article or a letter, and mailing to a friend ("Thought you would be interested . . ."). Valuable side effects include a more active reading of the news. Clipping also helps build the confidence that comes from being informed; it develops the ability to absorb major news trends, and it eases a sense of isolation.

Research

Make use of public facilities for research. The library reference department can provide names and addresses of company officials, as well as sources for practically anything. A postcard to your congressman or legislator will produce copies of bills and other governmental material. The League of Women Voters and Chambers of Commerce have up-to-date material on officials and government structure.

Recordkeeping

Keep a notebook with notes from meetings, daily lists of "to do's," and names, phones, and addresses of all contacts for future reference. A community activist will find a card file essential. Each card provides not only the above data but also includes brief notations about the person to jog the memory. Save lists of people, noting their interests. Such information is invaluable for all types of organizational activities, mailing lists, references, and as a source of committee members.

Make an outline

Whether for a letter, a report, a meeting, or a campaign, it's much easier to be creative and spontaneous if you have a structure on which to build.

Share

Letters, clippings, statements, and leaflets can do double duty if you share them with others interested. Useful exchanges result.

Fight guilt

Be more aware of what is accomplished than of what is not done. Enjoy, enjoy.

WOMAN'S WORK WILL YET BE DONE!

GALLERY OF PUT-IT-OFFS

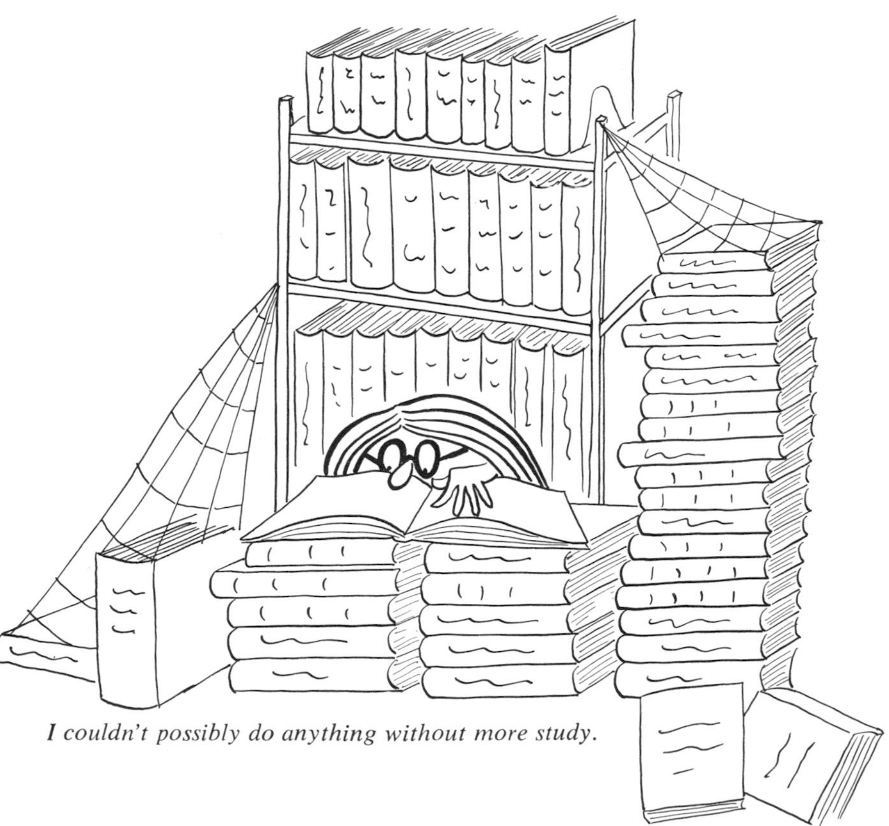

I couldn't possibly do anything without more study.

How can I write without my paper clips?
Just one more and I'll get to it.

Gotta get that last bit of dust.
I'll tackle the job when the kids are in bed.

5.
STARTING POINTS

Nobody starts from exactly the same place as anyone else, but we all have one thing in common: we have to start from where we are. So, look around and take good measure of yourself.

Where do I stand in regard to experience?

A woman had been a housewife and little else. She felt she could understand the frustrations and capabilities of other women like herself. She organized housewives to hold down the price of meat at the supermarket.

A can-smasher-and-bottle-returner enthusiast decided to apply her interest in recycling principles to community and national recycling movements.

What moves me?

A child injured by a defective toy was the impetus for her mother to become a safety-in-playthings activist.

A woman with a teen-age son approaching military age developed a community end-the-draft campaign.

After experiencing the frustrations of Medicare, a woman became deeply involved with alternative-health-service plans.

A young woman who had experienced an abortion worked hard on an abortion-repeal campaign.

What do I believe in? You must have at least a mustard seed's worth.

When a few citizens with faith were not discouraged by a series of defeats, a disheartened community was spurred on to block a freeway that would have cut through the neighborhood.

What do I want? Self-interest is about the strongest incentive of all.

A young woman with no calling for the usual female occupations and an intense interest in ecology could find no paid position in that field; she combined research and organization and eventually developed a project that was funded by a local foundation.

A feminist wanted to teach a course of woman's studies in a community college and be paid for doing it. She outlined such a course and convinced the administration to hire her.

What would I like to learn?

A person who enjoyed writing, but had little experience in it, took on the newsletter of an action organization, later turning it into a journal with reportage and comment.

With only the nagging desire to act, a woman joined a theater group with a social bent. She became a skilled performer.

What might work for me? One person's fulfillment is another's poison.

In a class of twelve women interested in activism, each was set in motion in a different way. One worked with welfare recipients. Another organized a fashion show recycling old clothes, and some put their efforts into revitalizing the organizations to which they belonged. After some shifting around, each found a direction that suited her particular circumstances.

Start in whatever way best moves you. Action is a line, not usually straight, from where you are to where you are going.

Housewives' Handicap System for Ego-Building

(For use only by housewives with poor self-images.*)

For being female in a male-run society .	10 points
If housewife, any action counts double, considering the difficulties . . .	20 points (average)
For being a self-motivator when everyone tells you not to bother	10 points
For keeping after it, despite the putdowns	15 points

* 97.9 percent, according to poll.

Over 35? You are supposed to be over
the hill . . . . 20 points

Now you can compete on even grounds, with anybody.

What-Is-My-Thing Inventory for Getting Started

Paper and pencil out again, be as specific as possible. Probe.

1. What do I enjoy doing most?
2. What am I especially good at?
3. What would I like to learn to do that I can't do now?
4. What are my strong qualities?
5. What limitations (physical, time, hours, transportation, etc.) must I take into account?
6. If I had my way, I would like to see the following changes in my community (nation):
7. Is there anything I could do to bring about any of above?
8. Which of my special skills, talents, or qualities could be used in so doing?
9. Where could I start?
10. What do I hope to gain for myself?

WARNING: If your inventory comes out something like this—

> I am lazy; I just can't seem to get anything accomplished, can't finish a task. I'm too emotional, get upset easily, nervous, no self-confidence, can't seem to carry things through

—you have the symptoms of a common ill, "housewive's paralysis." Read Betty Friedan's *Feminine Mystique* for a detailed description of its causes and symptoms.

For brown, red, and black versions of the same malady, substitute terms such as: shiftless, non–goal-oriented, unmotivated, no sense of time, emotional, illogical, immoral, biologically different (inferior).

A large number of us have been put down too long!

Kid, today you are just not my thing.

6.
PUSH-UPS TO GET STARTED

Push-ups are practice in activism. When a long-suffering consumer complains that a product does not live up to expectation, she becomes an unsilent American. As a TV viewer, she learns to talk back to the television set. As a citizen, she demands more voice than a few minutes each year in a polling booth. She is stating her position; she is participating in democracy.

Push-ups are the small assertions we make—the letter to a congressman, telephone call to a stranger, return of a purchase that was falsely advertised—any act that says, "I am a person, and this is how I stand." What good will they do? Whatever they may or may not accomplish on the receiving end, the woman who is flexing her muscles will be standing straighter. Push-ups are useful not only for starters; they can become a habit. They keep us in fighting trim, and they often lead us to longer-term projects.

Examples of Push-ups

A television viewer keeps postcards and pen near her set. When she sees something of which she strongly approves or disapproves, she writes the sponsor before the impulse dies.

Seeing a book review in her field of interest, a woman calls her library. If the book is not available, she urges its purchase.

A newspaper reader, angry at some outrage, clips the offending item, circles it, and writes a note: "Shame on you for . . ." She then mails it to the appropriate party.

When paying bills, a woman encloses a note: "I would like to see more women and persons from minority races in policy-making positions."

One feminist carries a stamp and stamp-pad in her purse. When she sees a vulnerable sexist poster, she leaves her educational mark on it: THIS INSULTS WOMEN.

A mother, concerned about an upcoming Board of Education hearing on a controversial busing plan, calls a community-minded TV station and suggests live coverage.

A shopper speaks to a store manager about a detergent on the shelf packaged in such a way as to be dangerous to small children. She then writes to the Food and Drug Administration about it.

Fed up with parties at which people segregate themselves by sex, a wife wears a Woman's Liberation button to such gatherings. Conversation becomes livelier, with both sexes participating.

An ecology-minded shopper removes excess packaging from a purchase, returns it to the store, and asks the management to pass her protest concerning the needless waste on to the manufacturer.

A pair of pantyhose that develops a premature run is returned with a letter to the manufacturer and a carbon copy to Virginia Knauer, the President's Adviser on Consumer Affairs. (Mrs. Knauer has expressed concern about faulty pantyhose.)

A camping enthusiast never fails to ask any forest ranger, "How many women are employed in this park?"

Sick about oil spills, a woman returns her credit card to the offending company, enclosing a letter explaining her position.

Having received unsolicited pornographic material through the mail, an angry woman writes for information on how to deal with this problem to Consumer Advocate, Office of the Postmaster General, Washington, D.C. 20260.

A mother who feels her children have too little exposure to other cultures takes a bibliography of children's books that presents varied backgrounds to the school librarian and discusses the problem with her.

A TV-commercial hater, irked by a particularly far-fetched claim, writes the Federal Trade Commission in Washington, D.C.: "Is it really true that . . ." (The Commission has been especially concerned with nutritional claims recently.)

A peace advocate always shops with her list of major war suppliers. She checks with the sales person to insure that she avoids these manufacturers.

What do things like these achieve? Considering the size of the problems, aren't they too insignificant to be worth the effort?

Remember, this is just the beginning. No matter how concerned with a problem, how well-read, or how articulate, few women have made serious attempts at trying to change that which bothers them because WOMEN ARE RELATIVELY POWERLESS.

Each push-up sets an example that will be followed by others, whether that was the original intent or not. Most important——one thing leads to another.

SURVEY
I'M MAKING A SURVEY. COULD YOU TELL ME HOW MANY WOMEN WORK HERE AND IN WHAT CAPACITY?
MR. DIMWINKLE, SIR DOES THE CIVIL RIGHTS ACT COVER US?
I HEAR THEY'RE AFTER THE BOSS TO UPGRADE WOMEN~THINK I'LL ASK FOR A PROMOTION.
WHY NOT APPLY AT MY PLACE? THERE'S TALK OF HIRING MORE WOMEN.

Escalating a Push-up

An innocent push-up can turn into a campaign if there is follow-through. For example:

PUSH-UP: A woman recently separated from her husband applies for a bank credit card in her own name. Because of her marital status, she encloses detailed proof of above-average economic resources.

RESPONSE: Form letter: "We regret we are unable to approve . . ."

PROBE I: She writes back: "I would be most curious to know the basis for your decision and the nature of the report. I understand I have this right under the Fair Credit Reporting Act."

NO RESPONSE: She waits three weeks without an answer. A common technique to cool a grievance is to slow down communication.

PROBE II: She visits the bank manager to follow up his offer of service after she opened her account.

ILLUMINATING RESPONSE: He is very conciliatory. "They just place people in categories A, B, and C. C—that's bad risks—includes separated or recently divorced women—just women, not men. It's not fair, I know. Maybe Women's Lib will do something about it someday. Just fill out another application, and I'll see if I can't get it through for you." She thanks him, but she decides that the principle is more important than the credit-card convenience.

PROBE III: She writes to the credit-data corporation mentioned in the first response: "Please consider this formal request, in writing, to know the nature of the report you made to (bank) that would result in my being denied credit." She sends a carbon copy to the bank administrator who turned down her application.

CONNECT: She sends copies of her correspondence to a sympathetic feminist lawyer.

PICKUP: The lawyer, talking to credit men about the problems of divorced women, uses this example to good effect.

ALTERNATIVE ACTIONS: Together, they discuss possible routes

to best change the discriminatory credit treatment of women:
(1) Write this up as a case study for a law review?
(2) Send a delegation of women's-rights activists to the bank?
(3) Prepare legislation to be offered to a sympathetic woman legislator for the next session?
(4) Write letters to women's organizations detailing the problem and suggesting action?
(5) Sue?

In this way, a push-up of a personal nature has turned into a group action. The issue of credit is one fragment of the larger whole: Equality for women. The person who started the ball rolling identifies her own credit status with that of all women in similar circumstances, and she carries the grievance forward as far as she can go—hopefully, until the inequality is rectified.

7. WRITE ON!

It used to be that when a woman objected to an injustice, she was told to write to her congressman. Since she seldom saw any result except a polite reply, letter-writing seemed like a meaningless exercise in futility. Now that women are on the move, skilled letter-writing is one more technique to make waves. In conjunction with other tactics, it has special virtues.

Its first virtue is availability. Anyone, anywhere, can do it with little effort, after the first few times. Second, it clears thinking and is good practice for convincing others. Third, because it is traditional, it is an excellent starting place for women unused to more direct action. Fourth, when timing is right, one well-placed letter can get the job done.

PUSH-UP POLLY

Comments from the Receiving End

§ *From a book publisher:* "Your comments are good ones with which we agree. . . . Your views will be made available to the author and editor for planning future books."

§ *From a legislative assistant:* "One handwritten letter is worth 500 to 1,000 postcards. We can tell a form letter from a personal one easily."

§ *From a senator's aide:* "Be sure it's clear where you stand and write about one thing only in a letter."

§ *A TV community-relations worker states:* "We're very sensitive to changes of 'climate.' Not all letters are answered, but they're read carefully."

§ *A politician's letter-answerer says:* "Every telegram must be signed for, read, and officially noted. We don't always have time for personal answers, but contents of each letter are recorded."

§ *A church group writes:* "Thank you for sending the material. Could someone from your organization come to talk to our group . . ."

To Whom?

§ *The President* (or Chairman of the Board). The *man* at the top makes most decisions. The library reference department usually can get you his name and address.

§ *Commissions and boards.* They receive relatively few letters, so ours may affect decisions. One letter addressed to a board is usually duplicated for individual members.

§ *Editors.* Become a columnist by writing a letter to the editor. You couldn't afford to buy comparable space in a newspaper or magazine. Comment on current issues, other letters, or introduce a new subject.

§ *Program managers.* TV depends on polls and public reaction. Send copies to sponsors.

§ *Educators.* Write teachers, principals, superintendents, deans, provosts. Curriculum, teaching methods, and personnel are all suitable subjects.

§ *Churchmen.* Change will occur when members suggest innovations in program, personnel, structure, or policy. Point out discrepancies between principles and practice.

§ *Businessmen.* As a customer, you are a VIP. As a stockholder, a boss. You have the right (responsibility) to ask, suggest, complain, and strongly recommend.

§ *Friends.* Letters, with or without clippings, widen the circle of involvement, as well as maintain personal ties.

WRITE TO WHOM IT MAY CONCERN.

Types of Letters

§ *To make an inquiry.* "The massive clear-cutting of those forests seems to this observer to show a complete disregard for the coming generation. What agency is supposed to regulate it? Is there anything that private citizens can do?"

§ *To make an acquaintance.* "Let me introduce myself as a new constituent in your district and congratulate you for your co-sponsorship of . . ."

§ *To encourage constructive action.* "If the board utilizes this rare opportunity to develop a working relationship with a community with severe educational problems, instead of feeling threatened by it, all of us will have gained. This is the only path out of our urban crisis."

§ *To expose hypocrisy.* "How can a city the size of San Francisco possibly afford to give the children of Chinatown a pool of such enormous dimensions? From the looks of it, it just might hold ten kids at a time."

§ *To call attention to problems ignored ("Yes, but . . .").* "As a stockholder, I have been reading your reports with interest. They are well-presented and appear forward-looking. However, I find nothing to indicate any concern or involvement with environmental or urban problems. I understand that . . ."

§ *To offer a solution.* "Six billion dollars needed to clean up the environment? Why all the hand-wringing when the answer is simple: Just close all tax loopholes. That will net the government $7.25 billion each year, leaving $1.25 billion for other good works."

§ *To express outrage.* "So the Senate had the gall to pass the ——— bill. Well, I certainly hope that you voted against it. How anyone can justify this special-interest piece of legislation, then talk economy when it comes to health and welfare programs, is beyond my understanding."

§ *To support a fighting candidate.* "When all of us who are dispossessed can see our common ground and our common foes at last, we may be on our way to accomplishing something. Thank you for renewing my hope that the ballot box might be one way to do so."

§ *To join a controversy.* "Read your letter suggesting that women give up their jobs to the returning veterans. Most women also work to support themselves and their families. . . . Besides the many female heads of household, married women often work because one salary can't keep up with inflation. What we really need is more jobs . . ."

§ *To keep nagging.* ". . . all those millions upon millions of plastic bags. They are used such a short time and take years to decompose. It's all terribly disheartening. We take one baby step forward ecologically and three steps back . . ."

§ *To ask why.* "If our scientists are so learned and intelligent that they can make nerve gas, why can't they be equally learned and intelligent and unmake it instead of polluting our oceans?"

Carbon Copy

If you want to be taken seriously and have real clout, if you want to be sure of an answer, if you want the most mileage for your letter, send copies to "the boss" and others concerned.

Locate the closest and cheapest Xerox machine and have copies made lavishly. In the bottom left-hand corner put: "cc: John Doe, President" (or whomever). For examples:

§ A letter of complaint to a commission appointed by the mayor.

cc: His Honor

§ A letter to a congressman.

cc: (a sympathetic organization of his constituents)

§ A letter to a sponsor about a TV commercial.

cc: the president of the company manufacturing the product (Call the library reference department for his name.)

§ Letter to a store about advertising, a consumer matter, or hiring practices. (Call the switchboard, get name of company's president, and write to him directly.)

cc: organizations of potential customers

§ Letter about any action taken.

cc: other groups that might back you up

Sample Letter

Senator (your district)
Senate Office Building
Washington, D.C. 20515

Dear Senator ———:
Please support Senator Bayh's amendment to S659, the Higher Education Act of 1971. It is vital that sex discrimination in universities and colleges be ended, and obviously it will take legislation to do so, since tradition is difficult to overcome.

Sincerely yours,

cc: [local] Federation of Women's Clubs

Note: The senator's aide will record that an activist constituent is watching and informing other voters. You will receive an answer. Send the carbon copy to the organization. You might like to add a cover letter explaining it.

Sample Cover Letter

Dear Friends: (or address it by name to the president. Lists are available at the Chamber of Commerce)

> Enclosed is a copy of a letter I sent recently to Senator ———, and some additional information about the Higher Education Act of 1971. Knowing the interest of your organization in educational opportunities for women, I am sure you will join me in urging passage of this legislation. Letters at this time—both personal and organizational—would be of great help.

When you just want to inform others, but not the addressee, about your action, send "blind" carbon copies; that is, put no notation on the bottom left-hand corner, but send a copy anyway.

AND BE SURE TO MAKE A COPY FOR YOUR FILE!

Escalating a Letter

A strong letter can turn into a campaign by extending its reach. For example:

STIMULUS: A woman reads a moving and factual article comparing war expenditures to costs of child-oriented programs.

RESPONSE: Using excerpts, she prepares a "Letter to the Editor."

EXTENSION: She mimeographs 150 copies and signs each personally. She mails them to the leading daily newspapers in all fifty states (names and addresses selected from N. W. Ayer's Directory of Newspapers, available at the library).

RESULT: A considerable number of newspapers reprint her letter. Her readership is in the hundreds of thousands.

8.
VOLUNTEER BEWARE!

Suburban Glossary

"I want to do something useful." I feel lonely and sad.

"I like to work with others." Maybe I need occupational therapy.

"Why don't you volunteer for something?" I hope it takes your mind off yourself.

"If you think the schools are so bad, why don't you help? They need tutors, you know." That ought to shut her up!

Volunteer work is the traditional safety valve for women, but very often a volunteer assignment seems like more of the very same old problems and frustrations of home.

Most volunteer work for women is low-skilled, repetitive, and unstimulating, as well as unpaid—home away from home. These tasks are sold to the volunteer on the strength of the psychic wages she will receive. She will be relieved of guilt because she will be fulfilling her "social responsibility." She will feel needed, useful, unselfish, appreciated, helpful—in general, reassured that she's okay.

Feminists are urging a hard look at the way in which volunteerism reinforces the helpmate tradition.

> Just as the feminine mystique is an ideology which has concealed the actual meaning of the housewife role, so the volunteer mystique conceals from our view that most service-oriented volunteerism:
> —serves to reinforce the second-class status of women;
> —is one more instance of the ongoing exploitation of women;
> —takes jobs from the labor market, and therefore divides middle class from poor and working women;

—buttresses the structures which are keeping women in a subordinate role;
—is antithetical to the goals of the feminist movement and thus detrimental to the liberation of women.

So states a NOW * position paper on "Women and Volunteerism."

Still, unpaid work *is* needed. Few projects for social change would get off the ground without it, and working without pay can provide valid psychic wages for everyone, male and female. The excitement and good feeling of a project shared, particularly when there are openings for creativity, are usually hard to match in the workaday world. Sometimes learning opportunities and apprenticeships can be found only in a non-paid situation.

Because so much of the traditional volunteer role needs critical reexamination and change, no woman should accept an unpaid assignment without first asking herself: Do I really want to do this? Why am I doing it? What do I expect in return? And, hopefully, more and more women will ask: Should this job be paid?

Volunteer Traps

Here are a few common volunteer traps to avoid:

Trap I: The Lady Bountiful. Not so common as it used to be, but many church groups still dutifully perform an annual good deed. This is most often engaged in by groups that wish to give a charitable veneer to their social gatherings. A common version is time-consuming fund-raising activity "for charity." Shun it.

Trap II: The Disadvantaged (*Lady Bountiful Recycled*). Not too many years ago, especially in the heyday of the "war on poverty," there was a strong urge by whites to want to "help," especially in the ghetto. Implied was: "*You* are helpless; I'm strong. You are inferior; I am superior. You're disadvantaged; I'm advantaged" (a fancy term for the same old White Man's Burden). Service was offered with the unexpressed hope that the

* National Organization for Women.

recipients would stay in "their" neighborhoods and "their" schools. Of course, it was resented. Then followed the equally popular "I was going to help (that is, volunteer in this or that program for the disadvantaged) but *they* didn't want us," which is the other side of the same helping coin. The white colonial pulls out and leaves the mess that he has created for the black man and woman to solve. The third alternative—fighting racism (working *with* non-whites to overcome the restrictive institutions)—has never been so popular. It means shouldering some of the burden, feeling some of the pain, experiencing a part of the ostracism that is the lot of minority people in white America. Key question to ask to avoid the *Disadvantaged Trap:* Am I only applying Band-Aids and expressing sympathy, or am I working on the problem? Avoid jobs that are only "service to the less fortunate."

Trap III: Scab Jobs. Unwittingly, many well-meaning women are doing more harm than good to the very persons they want to serve by giving away their labor. Their tasks often can be performed as well or better by people desperately in need of work. Part-time jobs especially are in short supply. There are so few available for elderly people who can't work a full day, for poor women with children, and for youth in school. The "war on poverty" proved that the poor can do effective service in their own communities. Older people could also work with the elderly, gaining new self-respect and a livelihood at the same time. Poor women could perform ably many of the functions that volunteers now do.

The immediate response to the idea of paying for volunteer services is: "There's no money for that in the budget; the services would have to be curtailed." But were there no volunteers around to perform necessary duties, adjustments would be made the next time the budget came up for review. Administrative and professional salaries might have to be pared, or new sources of funding explored. As a matter of fact, volunteers are often more essential to the administrators than to the recipients of their services. It is not uncommon for an administrator to say to a worker, "I could get a volunteer to do that," in the same way that employers have said, "I could get a woman for your job." Questions to ask: Could the work be done by a paid paraprofessional—someone who really needs a job, full or part time? If so, how could that be brought about?

Try to cut through the thick veil of benevolence that surrounds volunteerism and ask yourself frankly: What's in it for me? Unless there is a valid "selfish" reason, there is likely to be a hidden "unselfish" one that, when brought to light, is revealed as a desire to conform, a sense of personal inadequacy, or status seeking. The need to feel better than someone else is a by-product of stifled self-fulfillment. Giving may be more blessed than receiving, but sharing is healthier. Questions to ask: What can I offer? What will I gain? Avoid an unequal bargain.

Trap IV: Glamour Snare. A liberal public broadcasting station has an annual fund-raising auction. In preparation, brigades of volunteers (mostly women and a few hapless husbands) spend countless hours collecting merchandise. They are "rewarded" by being allowed to volunteer more hours at the prestigious event itself, where the TV camera may bring them into view for their children and babysitters at home. Question to ask: Do I really want vicarious glamour?

Trap V: The Generalissimo. Many of the worthiest-sounding causes are volunteer traps for women. You receive a professionally written brochure describing a particular social ill, and you are first asked to donate to an organization dedicated to correcting it. If you check a box saying you would be willing to become an active participant, you will later be contacted and given tasks that are essentially nothing more than fund raising and promotion, with little, if any, opportunity to participate in the decision-making process. Such organizations (some of which do important work) are pyramids, with unpaid female labor at the bottom. Question to ask: Is this the best use of my time? Usually it is not.

Trap VI: Woman's Place. The classroom mother calls—it's your turn to bake the birthday cake. Solicitors are needed for the Heart (Muscular Dystrophy/March of Dimes/Cancer/ United Fund) annual fund drive. Could you drive a group of children to the museum? Make something for the bake sale? "Man" a booth? Call the membership? Say yes once, and you're tabbed: "Try Mrs. Smith; she'll do it." A conscientious mother of a large family who belongs to a church and a PTA and believes in doing her duty could spend every moment extending unpaid household tasks to fill community needs. This is women's work carried to a *reductio ad absurdum.* Questions to ask: Is this my bag? If not, a well-rehearsed NO is in order.

Valid Volunteering

On the other hand, suppose you live in a suburban community, are convinced you want to do something about ghetto (Chicano/ Native American) problems, have had little contact with the people, and have no idea how to go about working *with* black (brown/ red). On inquiry you may learn that volunteers are welcome to help in a health center. *If* approached as in-service training for the bigger job of getting at the roots of the problem, such service can be educational and useful. The work is incidental; mainly it provides an opportunity to build empathy through firsthand experience. Don't go as an observer to see how the poor live, as if you are going to a zoo. Go to learn and be useful at the same time. Such work should be seen as temporary, as primarily for self-education, and done only on request of bona fide organizations of the community.

For example, a ghetto community-action program had planned a Saturday workshop for welfare recipients called "Public Welfare—Private Pain." One black organizer requested some volunteers for registering people, serving lunch, and helping out in the nursery—modest, "female" labor, with black and white women working together. The work was traditional, but participation in such an event provided the white volunteers with a glimpse of black community self-help and insight into a different style of work.

Some women will identify deeply with another culture, especially if they feel there has been unjust treatment. Over a period of time, they find their own ways to contribute to people struggling upward. Often they can provide a bridge to communicate with the dominant culture, but this is quite different from ministering to the downtrodden. The first becomes a donor-recipient relationship; the other, an alliance.

One woman with Chicano friends and some knowledge of how to prepare a funding proposal was useful in initiating a six weeks' training institute for Chicano students. Her experience was put to the service of a group who carried the proposal forward into an exciting project.

Another valid premise for volunteering is to create paid jobs for those who really need them. Often pilot programs do this. Some innovative projects will get underway with minimal funding, relying on the enthusiastic labor of volunteers. It is hoped that government or foundation funding will be forthcoming. However, grants, if any, too often are smaller than desired, and unpaid women remain in service. The goal of most volunteer assignments of this sort should be to work oneself out of a job in as short a time as possible.

In general, tackling the causes of social ills is better than treating the symptoms, although admittedly the dividing line sometimes blurs. The woman who spends countless hours mashing cans, cleaning bottles, and returning paper bags is really only daubing on Mercurochrome. What else can she do? At least she is setting an example, isn't she? Hopefully, she will begin to demand, in unison with like-minded people, that "something be done" by government, by manufacturers, by supermarkets. In the same manner, the medical-center volunteer can use her experience and motivation to spark health action. The nursery helper may work for childcare legislation.

With relatively few challenging paid jobs open to women, volunteerism does have its advantages. You can gain valuable new experiences; you can pick and choose, arranging convenient hours, learning new skills, and, if you like, preparing yourself for later employment. For some, it provides the only avenue open for self-actualization. The trick is to use the system, not be used by it.

V.V. Test (for Valid Volunteerism)

1. Will it enrich my life?
2. Does it fit into my own priorities?
3. Is it more a social changer than a social pacifier?
4. Does it avoid the traps?
5. If I accept, will the workload escalate out of sight?
6. Is my decision made of my own free will, or because I can't think of a good reason to refuse?

9.
NEW CAREERS FOR VOLUNTEERS

One of the more innovative approaches that emerged from the "war on poverty" in 1965 was the proposal to develop meaningful careers, not merely jobs, for the poor. A considerable number of paraprofessionals from the poverty ranks indeed did move into the "helping professions" (social service, teaching, recreation, and health services). Some of the underlying premises of this approach are quite applicable to women in all economic classes.

Establishing a goal. A poor person has no long-range goal. He or she is going nowhere in the job market, but lives on a day-to-day basis. *Parallel:* a housewife with children has little sense of a future in her own right. As a wife and mother, she has already arrived, although she may be very concerned about the future of her family. Establishing a stake in one's own future development has strong personal impact.

Sense of confidence. The changed self-image of a poor person moving up a career ladder is not unlike that of a housewife who begins to think: I am somebody after all. A step-by-step development sequence leads to a feeling of competence and self-worth.

Sense of belonging. Alienation is not restricted to the poor. Emptiness and lack of meaning are common to many housewives as well. The volunteer goes dutifully to the agency, performs each week the same act, knowing it is one tiny piece of a larger whole she never really sees. However, when she takes an active part in changing that whole, she participates not only in decision-making, but also in a creative process. A deeply felt cause makes life more exciting.

Relationship with professionals. The "New Careers" program sought to bridge the gap between professionals and the poor. As the program was conceived, the two were to work more as equals. Any volunteer who has been politely shunted to some make-work project knows the gap that exists between the "lady volunteer" and staff; behind-her-back ridicule is common. Moving up a ladder toward professionalism changes a volunteer's status to that of an intern or trainee, in the eyes both of her co-workers and herself.

Career Ladders Out of Volunteerism

Research. Programs for social change require increasing amounts of research. For example, Nader's Raiders and environmentalists now attack many problems through the legal system. Lawyers alone can't possibly do all the necessary investigation. If you are willing to learn how to use a law library, you can tackle issues dear to your heart in a manner likely to produce results. At the same time, you learn something valuable for yourself, which later might escalate into paid employment. Inquire at law schools or change-oriented legal societies about law research for laywomen. Some women attorneys would welcome volunteer assistance to handle the flood of feminist cases.

Researchers are needed wherever the future is being shaped, and they are by no means limited to law. Non-establishment medical groups, usually comprised of socially minded interns, medical students, and nurses, are experimenting with new forms of providing service to the poor. Such groups often conduct studies of health needs and might welcome volunteer researchers.

An example of a "new breed of research army . . . marching and multiplying" is the Council on Economic Priorities, which has offices in New York, Washington, and San Francisco. Teams of young volunteers investigate what corporations are doing in pollution control, minority hiring, and investments in foreign countries with repressive regimes. After extensive research, they rate companies' performance as members of society. One survey detailed how pulp-and-paper producers have responded to demands for a cleaner environment by means of a large advertising and press release campaign. ("It cost us a bundle but the Clearwater River still runs clear.") The Council charges for its reports, and has received tax-exempt status. There is a small, subsistence-paid staff augmented by students and volunteers.

Then there are feminist organizations that seek out women

willing to monitor and analyze television programs for sexist content. Inquiry into voting records of legislators is also in demand. All in all, research is a good volunteer ladder, because it can lead anywhere. It builds know-how and ego while it lays the basis for better things to come.

Organizing. Good volunteer organizers are needed in every area. A skilled one can almost write her own ticket. For a woman who likes to work with people and is willing to accept the ideas of others, this is a satisfying area that offers a chance to innovate in exciting ventures: there is a perennial shortage of behind-the-scenes leadership! Prepare step-by-step, in the same way as planning a career, moving from small to larger projects—testing, evaluating and studying. Eventually, you may work for pay.

Teaching. Adult teaching situations are on the increase. High school evening classes and college extension divisions offer constantly changing classes, as do YWCAs and community centers. Restless women throng to them. For the more adventurous, "free universities" offer such subjects as creative vacations, psychodrama, organic gardening, practical politics, and Zen. Feminist groups in some areas are organizing instructions in auto mechanics, self-defense, women in history, and family life—even breadmaking for the single woman. If teaching appeals to you, develop a specialty, work up a course, then find or create a place where it can be taught. While stimulating for the volunteer, it's also a learning situation that could lead to a paid position or fees.

Potential innovators in education for children have many opportunities. New approaches in experimental alternative schools are usually long on flexibility and short on paid staff. From volunteer experimentor to paid educator is a reasonable career ladder. Early childhood education, in particular, is a fast-developing field where a dedicated volunteer could prepare for a future position.

Drama and the arts. All the arts are essential to social change as well as to enjoyment of life. Small skit groups can educate as they entertain, sometimes as an adjunct to discussion. If this appeals, find the best one around, or gather together other interested persons. Don't expect excellence in the beginning, but work in that direction. Invite resource persons (anybody who knows more than you do) to help develop skills of director, writers, actors—learning as you go. The same with art. Take it seriously enough to point toward professionalism.

Media. Begin by taking on the newsletter of a local organization. It's a good place to learn the discipline of organizing ideas and communicating to others—and printing techniques. Move on to reportage or creative writing for any of the journals that are springing up, whether they pay or not. Perhaps take a class, if you find one sufficiently tailored to your interests. Explore the other media, too. More jobs for women are just becoming available in television and radio. Some stations are using volunteer apprentices, and this could be a good way to start. A related area that lends itself to a career ladder out of voluntarism is publicity, since numerous organizations would love to have you practice in their behalf.

Politics. For someone who likes the push and pull and is not easily intimidated, politics is wide open. Here, of course, one starts as a volunteer—but avoid, if possible, too much stamp-licking. To learn the ropes, work in a campaign with the candidate of your choice, gaining organizational experience and making contacts—the nub of politics. The more speaking you do, the better.

Most local governments have commissions or other citizen bodies that may be penetrated if one is willing to put in enough work to prove seriousness. Getting on is more who you know than what, so cultivate a friendship with a person who advises or determines appointments.

Fledgling women politicians can get assistance from the National Women's Political Caucus and its emerging state counterparts, and training at "Schools for Candidates" conducted by the National Organization for Women (NOW). Feminists are determined that what Congresswoman Bella Abzug derisively calls the House of Semi-Representatives will soon see more women in its halls. Might as well aim high. A recent Gallup poll finds that 66 percent of the electorate would now vote for a qualified woman for President. There's a ladder that's out of sight—or is it?

Ombudswoman. Bureaucratic–red-tape cutter is not yet an official profession in most places, but it is a coming one. There are many ways to get started in this business: for example, with welfare. Legal aid groups often use volunteers to support clients at hearings. The role is not that of a substitute welfare worker but that of an advocate who has studied the rules sufficiently to support the recipient. Welfare rights groups have also used dedicated volunteers to write materials that explain simply the tangle of regulations; their purpose is to ensure that the recipient receives what she is entitled to. Prison volunteers work in penal institutions for women as advocates of inmates.

The line between volunteerism of this sort and traditional services seems very fine because it is. However, the old style was helping an individual while leaving the institution intact. The new style moves beyond the individual to affect the way the institution functions. It should progress from mediating an individual complaint to insisting that the procedure be improved. Changes might include the volunteer's role as well; her job possibly could be converted into that of a paid agent of change.

In Sweden, where the office of ombudsman was created, it was recognized that, bureaucracies being what they are, someone has to intervene in behalf of the little guy. This sounds like a fine position for a woman.

Fund raiser. The scramble for money is intense, and those who can get it are in great demand. Besides organizing fund-raising campaigns, there is proposal writing and budget-making. There's no problem of getting started here. Just announce to any small organization you belong to that you would like to learn to be a fund raiser, and offer your services. Study as you go, learn from success and failure, and move up from the place where you have to do most of the work yourself. Or, turn professional.

Ecology woman. Successor to the handyman, this specialist would collect tips on recycling, information on regulatory agencies, and skills in repair. With some training in how-to-fix-it and a lot of imagination, she would soon become a neighborhood resource in great demand. She could change the emphasis of the current garage-sale craze from just moving the junk around to sensible reuse. She could help channel individual ecology efforts into pressure on the institutional roadblocks. Eventually she could, if so minded, generate income by the sale of materials, consultive fees, and charges for repairs.

Lobbyist. Only about .04 percent of California's professional lobbyists at the state capital are women, but times are changing! There are a number of other women who are volunteer lobbyists for a particular cause or for their organization (League of Women Voters or National Organization for Women, for example). For someone living near a local capital, here is a chance to get into the thick of things and learn by doing. First find that sympathetic veteran who is willing to train a newcomer. After the first encounters, the intrigue should be stimulating more than frightening. One ironic twist mentioned by professionals—legislators won't let "ladies" pick up the tab—means that a professional woman lobbyist's expense account can be much smaller than a man's. Since women have been advising men how to run things for generations, lobbying provides an opportunity to put that strength to use in a wider arena. Prediction: More jobs for capable, experienced women in this field.

Career ladders leading out of voluntarism must be tailored to the individual. Instead of: What can I do that's needed? (which generally ends up being what no one else wants to do), ask: What can I do where I can make the greatest contribution, learn the most, have a chance for advancement, and possibly prepare for a future career? How can I contribute to more fundamental change?

This is a big shift. There should be no shame or guilt in having a self-interest. It was always there in the old form, just hidden and more hypocritical. In the new approach, there is honest recognition that if you give your labor you expect a return. To realize this and anticipate real psychic rewards changes the volunteer role from a passive to an active one.

To anyone who says that looking forward to payment is potentially corrupting—of course it can be. Will we destroy the "selflessness" that is a feminine virtue? Will we assume all the worst features of the male rat race? Are we just interested in a bigger slice of the pie for ourselves? We can all point to women who have fought their way into "a man's world" on others' backs and have identified only with their own narrow, personal interests. Yes, that is something to be guarded against.

But most women have an exaggerated "selflessness" that limits the contribution they can make. Being paid, especially in our how-much-does-he-make society, changes the way we look at ourselves and how others see us. Co-workers may lavish praise on a volunteer, but are more likely to respect a professional. The woman who "doesn't need" the money can always plow her salary back into the cause or help to fund struggling projects. Furthermore, there will always be waves to make for free.

10.
VOLUNTEER POWER

On the other hand, women *are* volunteers. Any smart group starts where people are and uses whatever means are at hand; this leads to creative new tactics. In the wake of the Women's Liberation Movement, the formerly docile gender is utilizing courts, ballot boxes, media, and more direct challenges to upgrade woman's position. Still untried is the enormous potential of volunteer power. Aristophanes's Lysistrata stopped a war by organizing women to withhold that which men desired most. Consider what would happen if a significant portion of unpaid female workers were to call it quits! Political campaigns would come to a grinding halt; fund raising would stop in its tracks, and most "good causes" would flounder until demands were met.

This is not to propose a volunteer strike, but to point out the power that volunteers possess to affect change. Women who work at a paid job can't risk offending management so easily. On the other hand, a volunteer has little to lose. She's not risking her livelihood, and there are always plenty of openings for unpaid labor.

When a volunteer is unhappy about the use of her time, the way the program is run, or anything else, she just drops out. Turnover is tremendous, as any coordinator will testify. Would it not be more fruitful for dissatisfied volunteers to band together? Even a small delegation to the powers that be could have an affect.

Take the Pledge

Dorothy Samuel of Baltimore, an individual with initiative, wrote to leading women's organizations as follows:

> Ever since southern women defied the law to teach the first slaves to read and write—while advanced white males were making speeches—the women of this nation have been the active troops in every educational, charitable, civic, libertarian,

> religious and other good cause. From the overworked farm wives who raised the money for the pastor's salary to the suburban women who stuff envelopes for reform political candidates to the college girls who march in every demonstration for brotherhood or peace, the women have been the working core in every altruistic endeavor. We have raised the money, canvassed by telephone, served the food, gotten out the mailings, pounded the typewriters, filled the streets, manned the service projects—and fed and comforted the males afterwards as they relaxed from facing the TV cameras and making the decisions. LET'S CALL A HALT!

She proposes that more women serve in decision-making positions. In addition, a serious attempt should be made to bring men into volunteer roles formerly assigned to females. Organizations that want women's support should pledge to bring the sexes into better balance.

Sample Letter

> Gentlemen:
> I am responding to your recent request. This is not due to any change in my concern for your goals and activities. However, in concert with thousands of American women, I am withdrawing my support—my contributions of both time and money—from all groups continuing to discriminate against women in positions of leadership. Your letterhead, signatories, and representatives have not shown women in proportion to the numbers of women rendering service and support through the years.
>
> I hope that this discrimination has been an inadvertent oversight with you, brought about by unthinking acceptance of the general mores of our society. . . .

Ms. Samuel is calling for women to use their volunteer power in their own interests. As in every other human endeavor, don't complain—organize!

Take a look at a typical Volunteer Bureau ad. If we had real compassion, we would insist that these needs be met through ade-

Volunteer Bureau

A member agency of the United Crusade.

Chat-ter. If you enjoy conversation, we've got people who'd like to talk to you. After work or during the day, you could help someone practice English. Be someone's English conversation partner. You'd be working in a program that has already helped a good many people to qualify for jobs, to buy groceries, and just to function in a world that has been foreign to them.

A fine part-time job for an older woman.

Ichthyology enthusiast. The Ichthyology Department of a science foundation needs someone with both brawn and brains to help organize their fish collection and see that the aquariums are properly cleaned periodically. The job entails lots of lifting and carrying and scurrying around. A high school or college man would be perfect.

If no one volunteers, next research grant will include money to pay for this.

Bailer-Outers. People are needed to interview prisoners. Gather information that will be considered for getting them released from jail on their own recognizance.

A chance to learn something here. Passes VV test.

Volunteers Needed

Morale booster. Blood bank needs someone to greet donors, serve hot coffee and thank people for coming.

How about a little reinbursement for the grandmother. It would do wonders for her morale.

Personnel/Social Work Background.

You don't absolutely need professional training to handle this job. But it would be helpful. A few well-qualified volunteers are needed to interview families who want to provide Foster homes.
We also need volunteers with special capabilities to help consumers who feel they've gotten a bad deal from someone. Register complaints

Good part time work for women going back to school for social work.

Pediatrics helper. To tell stories, tend teddy bears, and tousle heads in a children's ward. Anyone from a teenager to a grandmother could be good at this.

More men volunteering will balance things out somewhat.

TEACHERS' AIDES

As you know, classes are getting larger in our public schools. Teachers' loads become heavier each year. So volunteers are being brought in from the community to help out. And they're really helping. But there aren't nearly enough of them. If you volunteer, you'll be working one-to-one with students, maybe even taking over a reading group for a couple of hours each week. The teacher you help will be able to spend more time teaching. And you're bound to enjoy the hours you spend in the classroom.

Paid para-professionals from similar backgrounds as the students are more effective, more consistent, and THEY NEED THE WORK.

Child lover. Various day-care centers in the Bay Area need someone to tell stories, sing lullabies, tie endless shoelaces. You'll get paid in nothing but love.

How about child-care for your own kids in return.

quate funding, which in turn would create the jobs so badly needed. Let's indeed do something . . . for change!

Do Something . . . for Change

VOLUNTEERS NEEDED

Pricewatchers in supermarkets. Vigilant checkers to assist consumer group hold the price line.

RESEARCHER

Someone willing to study and digest all available material on noise abatement. Interested citizen group needs information for testimony before City Council.

Conservationist. Experience in organizing a letter-writing campaign. To save wild river area. Lots of willing help, none willing to take responsibility.

Wanted: testimony from parents who have had bad experience with unsafe toys. Also obscene ones that present psychological hazards, such as sadism. Crusading team is preparing testimony and needs additional evidence.

Attention Senior Citizens

Consultants needed for planning retirement home. Be prepared to offer opinions on style of architecture, neighborhood facilities needed. Willing to work with planners and architects, as well as decorators.

ARE YOU INVENTIVE?

Suggestions needed for an alternative to plastic containers for various products. Ecology groups welcome any ideas.

Picketers. Numerous openings depending on special interests of applicants. Acute shortage of persons willing to express convictions in this manner. Opportunity to meet others of like persuasion.

Eco-activists Attention. Ten persons needed to test effects of putting bricks in toilet tanks. Must be willing to go beyond individual action to help develop program for alternative disposal of human waste.

Proposal writer. Grass roots community group is investigating potential for Cable TV to provide a voice for a powerless minority.

School for paramedics. Training for medical assistants, transcriber, secretary, claims examiner, management adm. asst., surgical technicians, blind medical transcribers, and other growing specialties. Train now for paid positions. Volunteer exp. useful.

RACISM

Expert needed for curricula development. Must be ready to work in conflict situation.

Court Watch. Learn the justice system from the inside and provide a service as you learn. Legal society will train you to watch for inequalities under law.

Like to Type?

Really? Many openings in all kinds of causes. To avoid being *typecast* insist upon opportunity to contribute in other areas.

Women with preschool children. Cooperative childcare project now in formation. Working toward funded program.

HISTORIAN

To prepare materials for Susan B. Anthony day exhibits in library. Imaginative person with research bent.

11.
VOCATIONS AND CAREERS FOR SOCIAL CHANGE

Vocations are different from careers. Curious, but women are generally said to have careers when they work, such as "career women attention: saleswomen, secretaries, waitresses . . . ," or "career clothes for the clerical force." On the other hand, one doesn't refer to bricklaying as a career. Or automechanics.

Most women who work choose a vocation that is open to females, is one they can "relate to," has some measure of security, and does not involve too much hassle. But TIMES ARE CHANGING. There's hardly an employment field where some woman is not saying, "Why not? Why can't women be bricklayers?" Not *all* women, but that one bricklaying nut who learned by helping her father build a house. She demands to be considered as an individual, not as a member of a disadvantaged (weaker) group.

With some of the law on her side, she decides to fight it through, but she is a real threat to the "natural order of things." The obstacles put in her way are enormous. If she wins, she may make *Time* magazine and receive accolades from feminists everywhere. For a woman, bricklaying is a career—or at least a vocation for social change. By her defiance of tradition and prejudice, she questions old shibboleths, batters down another closed door, and creates one new choice. She becomes a pace-setter.

At a conference I attended, a group of women were going around the circle giving their names and occupations. One said, "I have a body and fender shop." Everyone applauded.

But breaking into a man's field isn't the only vocation for social change. You can give new direction to an old career, or create a new one.

Lawyer

Salle Soladay is a thirty-five-year-old woman lawyer who is into prison reform. That's a field that is not new to women—in fact, it was women who initiated juvenile reforms way back. But with the crisis in today's prisons, a woman who is an advocate of the embattled inmates finds herself searching more deeply for causes and solutions. "I'm telling women, 'For gosh sake, get out of the kitchen and jump into the society. We need help.' " Salle Soladay started with a general law practice, but her heart and her hand pulled her into a new kind of kitchen that has plenty of heat.

With the civil rights movement for women, law schools are a mecca. Take this notice appearing in a feminist magazine:

> Women: make the movement. Become a lawyer. For information on women in law, on becoming a lawyer (you don't need a B.A. in California), applying to law school, and profiles of Calif. law schools' admission standards, write to the Boalt Hall Women's Assoc., University of Calif. School of Law, Berkeley, 94720.

Marcia Wilson, student at Boalt, said that feminism and the law have become intertwined for her. "You might say feminism is almost a way of life."

A law background is also a starting place for a political career or for becoming involved in society's problems. There, a woman can either become lost in the maze or define a new feminist direction.

Consultant

That's a nice, comforting title, implying that people will beat a path to your doorstep to ask your advice, and pay you handsomely for your wisdom. All this, and you can arrange your hours flexibly to conform with the rest of your interests as well. That's hard to come by, and takes the kind of ingenuity and drive that is rare. But not impossibly rare. As pressures for change grow stronger, women who have made themselves experts, women who have learned to write grant proposals, and women who are grounded in their "Movement" will be needed to help devise new structures. The childcare field, for example, will need such self-defined specialists.

Medics and other health workers

Women are pounding on the doors of medical as well as law schools. They are bringing with them new ideas on how doctors should function in society and what health is all about. Paraprofessional roles are also being considered. Midwifery is a new/old specialty that reflects the concern for women's control of their own bodies. Some doctors and community clinics are teaching the techniques. Also, nurses are conceiving of their function in some community clinics in new terms. Instead of being handmaidens to physicians, they participate in medical teams that consider all the nutritional needs of health-deprived citizens. Often they find themselves embroiled in struggles for surplus food and needed services. Cook County Hospital in Chicago has proposed a patient advocate to help patients utilize the services that are available as well as to mediate between patients and hospital.

Consumer advocate

Better-business bureaus have the distinct disadvantage of being financed by businesses they are supposed to regulate. With greater consumer awareness, the time is ripe for independent bureaus supported by private funding or subscriptions. A vigorous advocate would serve the public at large as well as save money for her clients.

Storekeeper

Don't expect to get rich running a woman's book store, or a craft store or an ecology shop. But for the subsistence-minded, it's a possibility that could be integrated into a larger circle of activities. The shop can be a communication center of a movement in a community. However, a word of caution: Many such enterprises fail because they are approached with illusions, or because staying power is insufficient.

Technological innovator

Now that sounds unlikely for a woman. But consider a field that is in its infancy—one that you might put your mark on. Like cable television.

Boat-rocker

Even the most traditional of women's fields can use innovators. But a person doesn't usually start out in that role. Often she is the critic who raises the embarrassing questions at the staff meetings or professional gatherings. "If you know what's good for you, you won't rock the boat," she is warned. Instead of being cautious, she reads about innovations going on elsewhere, talks to the most perceptive people in her field, perhaps risks the disapproval of her superior. All the time she focuses on the needs to be dealt with rather than the expediencies of the circumstances.

Despite the warnings, if she correctly assesses the coming changes, *and* if she has some support behind her, the likelihood is that she will be the one to move forward when innovation time comes.

12. BECOME AN EXPERT

Dianne Feinstein, as President of the San Francisco Board of Supervisors in 1971, spoke to a group of women who wanted to become active in politics. "Choose an area that interests you and become expert in it," she advised. Her choice was crime. She studied it, researched both theory and local practice, and made speeches wherever possible. From time to time, she was asked to testify on one measure or another, and she became known as a resource person in the field. She not only received press coverage, but also could speak with knowledge on an issue of vital interest to the electorate. In 1969, in her first try for elective office, when she ran for the Board of Supervisors, she topped the field of candidates and became president of the board.

Women are more often generalists than specialists, which, like most things, is both positive and negative. Unless she trains for a specific job, a woman is likely to pursue a broad course of humanistic study. If married, her home skills cover a wide range but seldom require much depth of knowledge. She is an amateur cook, chauffeur, nurse, psychologist, handywoman, housekeeper, sometimes bookkeeper, teacher, nursemaid, recreation director, community organizer, decorator, gardener, entertainer, negotiator, and usually a lot more.

This is all good experience, but never learning how to specialize is discouraging. Always in awe of the "experts," such a woman feels inadequate to lead. She is likely to relegate herself into the category of willing helper, the one who is always handed the drudgery.

How to Go About Becoming an Expert

Suppose you have had an unfortunate experience in a hospital. You had complications following uterine suspension surgery, which another doctor later claimed was unneccssary and endangered your life needlessly. You are now, more than ever, aware of the crisis in delivery of health care, and have been following the controversy in the media. Nobody has made a statement from the viewpoint of the medical customer that quite satisfies you, yet you know this is something that concerns everyone, one way or another. You decide to dig in.

Read

Libraries are always good starting places. Reference librarians must be born cooperative (very "womanly"). Do a selective job of reviewing the literature, bypassing overly technical treatises and out-of-date material. At first you may end up with nothing worth taking home but a few notes. (Who ever cared what the patient thought of health care?) Also check through current periodicals, disciplining yourself not to be distracted while scanning the table of contents. Don't miss the *Standard Periodical Directory*.

Bookstore browsing will reveal recent publications, either to purchase or to urge your librarian to purchase. Check book reviews for the newest muckraker.

Study

Are any courses at the community college remotely concerned with this problem? Lecture series? Call the local medical school; you may learn of meetings not generally publicized.

Collect

Start a clipping file of news releases, articles, letters, and anything else dealing with the issue. Buy or beg magazines with informative articles. Collect bibliography gleaned from all sources —especially current books and research. List names of people who are proposing legislation, testifying, making statements, writing letters, and the like—in other words, people who are also concerned and active, whatever positions they may take on the issue.

Listen

Attend meetings on your topic held by any group. Wherever possible, talk about the subject, ask questions, and listen carefully. Take notes. Begin to sort out the right questions even before you think you have the answers. Who is on what side? Why? Look for self-interest.

Exchange

Let others know your concern. Establish trade with people working in other fields. "I'll clip things for you on recycling if you will do the same for me on health care." Follow up leads. "Doris is writing a thesis on the topic in Public Affairs. She says she will be glad to send you a copy of a paper she wrote." Not only ask for it, but also establish a give-and-take relationship, in your mutual interest.

Tour

Firsthand research is the best kind. Sit in a hospital waiting room and engage in conversations. Visit a low-income area with a medical social worker to find out about health care in that setting. Talk with doctors, nurses, and administrators, for, while your primary concern is the medical consumer, the "industry" viewpoint is a necessary context. Don't miss medical students whose vision may still be fresh. When you discover significant case histories, not only record them, but also ask if the person would be willing to testify.

Write

Ask any legislator who has proposed a bill on the subject for a copy. Also write to any commission or other official bodies concerned (the library can supply addresses). When you are ready to take a position, do so in writing. Respond to statements in the paper with a letter to the editor; write to a sympathetic publication or newsletter. When ready, submit an article to a magazine.

Speak

Let it be known that you are available to speak on the subject, starting with smaller, less knowledgeable groups. ("I have been researching this issue, and I would be interested in sharing some of the information I have gained, as well as discussing the controversial aspects of the proposed legislation.") One speaking date leads to another, and also adds new contacts with others similarly interested. A TV station might like an interview.

Once you are an "expert," what have you gained? A new or refreshed grasp of how to go about gathering information. New confidence—you know, and others know—that you can take a subject seriously. Should you join an organization at this point, you do so with a specialty. If it appears more fruitful, you can bring together others of like mind for an ad hoc action. Or you can continue to work as an individual, perhaps as a resource person for legislation, writing, and speaking. *Or move up a career ladder.*

13.
WHAT ONE TURNED-ON PERSON CAN DO

A group is sitting around a cold campfire complaining because no one knows how to build a fire. Then somebody drops a match that ignites the tinder. It may just flicker and go out. On the other hand, there may be a scramble for more matches, drier tinder, and a pile of kindling. The individual act by a highly motivated person works like a match. We read daily of women like:

§ Lorena Weeks of Wadley, Georgia. Over six years ago she decided she would prefer the job of switchman for higher pay than continue her clerical job with Southern Bell Telephone Co. Turned down for the job, she sued. After six years of litigation, backed by the National Organization for Women, she won not only the job, but also $30,761.68 in back pay, overtime (made by the man who got her job in 1966), interest, and travel pay (to her clerical job). In other words, she got everything she lost, and didn't have to pay a lawyer's fee (under Title VII, losing companies pay). Her case became a model for other suits involving sex discrimination in employment. That back-pay ruling will make other employers hesitate, and encourages other women to dare apply for unlikely jobs. *Form of action: Court battle.*

§ Louise Bruyn of Newton, Massachusetts, walked 450 miles in 45 days to Washington, D.C. This dancing teacher had decided to make a personal protest against the Vietnam war. To the reporters and legislators who met her on the Capitol steps she brought messages from people she encountered along the way, the vast majority of whom, she said, wanted to end the war. *Form of action: Newsworthy feat.*

§ Dorothy Bradley of Gallatin County, Montana, is an ardent environmentalist. She decided that the best way to get people thinking and talking ecology was by running for office on that platform. She ran for the state legislature with the slogan "Dorothy is for the Birds and the Elk and the Bears and the Flowers and for Montana" displayed on campaign litter bags. She won, and is the only woman in Montana's House of Representatives. *Form of action: Political campaign.*

§ Elouise Westbrook, community activist, concentrates her efforts in the Hunters Point–Bayview area of San Francisco. As a woman who speaks out vigorously on every local issue, she gives backbone to her community. Battling red tape and bureaucrats, she fights for better housing, schools, health care, and human rights. She makes officials shudder with "We're watching your every step, baby." *Form of action: Community watchdogging.*

§ Helene Lippincott, also of San Francisco, spent six weeks in grocery stores deciphering food codes (symbols on perishable products to advise management when they should be removed from the shelves). She took this information to anti-establishment papers, which eagerly published it. A lawsuit on behalf of consumers was sparked by this act, which coincided with stepped-up consumer activities. Preferring to settle out of court, many dairies, bakeries, and market chains began clearly dating their products. Now, "October 4" means that spoilage may be expected by that date, and the product should be pulled. *Form of action: Reportage.*

§ Joyce Gallagher of Beverly Hills, California, developed the ultimate Christmas gift for a husband to give his wife: equality. Under current California law, community property is owned jointly by husband and wife, but the man has control of that property. He may manage it as he sees fit. Ms. Gallagher prepared a legal contract that equalizes that control. By Christmas of 1971, thousands of the contracts had been sold at the price of one dollar. Joe Gallagher, her husband, was the first customer. *Form of action: End run around an outdated law, a symbolic victory.*

§ Susan Davis of Chicago worked as a full-time volunteer in developing a black newspaper in Boston, and later as advertising manager. "My major interest turned toward developing minority businesses. Then I realized I was part of a minority, and that realization logically took me into Women's Liberation." Over a year ago she started *The Spokeswoman,* a monthly newsletter covering women's interests in employment, education, childcare, politics, life patterns, and much more. This is a badly needed catalyst to inform women as they move ahead. *Form of action: Uniting a movement by providing a communications vehicle.*

§ Anaïs Nin, writer of novels and a monumental diary that chronicles her own struggle for liberation, is at sixty-eight a model for young feminists. Her individual journey, from a strict Spanish Catholic background to rebellion and a gradual sense of identity, inspires young women who are traveling the same road. But now it is not so lonely. Ahead of her time, she learned to run a printing press in order to publish her own writings. Today each volume is eagerly awaited. *Form of action: Personal statement.*

Each of us has an orbit, some larger than others. We influence people around us, often without even knowing it. Sometimes

a woman tells me that I helped her get started, or that she learned this or that from some project we worked on together. Yet I was so intent on the project that I was not aware of the influence. All of us are constantly looking around for role models, but we ourselves can become them.

The crusades of the women above were diverse, as were their methods, but each set an example and kept plugging until something was accomplished. Each in her own way dropped a match.

Working in Groups

AN ANCIENT TALE

SOME VILLAGE WOMEN
WERE STUCK INSIDE
AN OLD DRY WELL

HELP
SOME OF THE WOMEN
TRIED TO GET UP BY
SCREAMING FOR HELP

SOME OF THE WOMEN
BY RUNNING & LEAPING
BY SHOVING & PUSHING

SOME BY PRAYER &
LAMENTS OF INFERIORITY
"WE'RE ONLY WOMEN"

AT LONG LAST ONE
WOMAN SAID "LETS
HELP EACH OTHER UP"

SO THEY ORGANIZED
AND HELPED EACH
OTHER UP.

14.
BANDING TOGETHER

This section is primarily about those groups we join in order to create social change. We want to be more effective, and wish to focus our energies into something that will produce results. Alone we feel helpless. All together, perhaps, we can get something done. But it's not all that simple . . .

The Long Road to Action

There seems to be a pattern for female involvement in groups. First, women are *concerned*. We see a problem. In many cases that's a big, broad, general problem, like war or the environment, or sexism. We feel strongly, but may not know, or don't think we know, much about it. So first we want to discuss it, study it, hear others speak about it—ad nauseum, according to the activists in the group. We may describe it as "becoming informed" if we are traditional, or "getting ourselves together" if in the counterculture. Action ideas at this stage find few takers, and impatient women may give up.

Then, when we feel at last we know, missionary zeal takes over, and we respond well to a call to spread the word. Speakers' bureaus flourish, newsletters and publications multiply. Fact sheets and position papers become increasingly articulate. Family and friends are brought into the debates.

Another phase is service. Women gravitate to this form of expression, because of our homemaker role. When we feel strongly about a problem we want to get right in and do something about it in a personal way. Some organize alternative structures, such as free medical centers, to demonstrate the way society ought to function. Also, these are seen as places to "radicalize" all who participate.

Some involved Women Liberationists are more internal in their approach. A woman's center will possibly provide counseling (rapping), women's small groups (rapping), crash pads, abortion referral, and perhaps communal child care. It may serve as an informational network to develop communication within the Movement. It symbolizes, and to a considerable degree provides, a sense of sisterhood, linking the individual woman with all others of like persuasion.

The service orientation is not limited to feminists, however. A penchant for can-crushing and bottle-washing, and formation of neighborhood recycling centers, is the ecologists' version. Women concerned with poverty and welfare work to set up a system for distribution of food stamps. A human relations council turns to fund raising for a minority self-help project.

WARNING: Unless the service project is an essential step to arouse people to action—unless it is a model for proposed change, or a necessary but shortlived phase for those participating—beware of Band-Aids that divert us from treating the sore beneath. Women may find themselves in the same old volunteer service roles with little accomplished.

The organization phase may turn people into by-law enthusiasts. Structure can become so engrossing that we find ourselves trying to devise rules that will take care of every contingency. Then we usually put the carefully prepared rules into a drawer, because life and action are just too complex.

Some women are trying to bypass organization mania, but it will probably catch up with them. This includes more than the knotty problems of building a structure, attracting a membership, and raising money. It means constructing a power base. Unfortunately, no one has come up with a substitute for organization, just new forms of getting it done.

Action usually—but not necessarily—comes last. After a group has talked and talked, and spoken out, and tried to serve, and organized itself in one way or another, it may be ready to act in a way that challenges the powers that be. Whether it is an action *against* some injustice or *for* a proposed change, whether it is a group letter of protest or a march downtown, the group has agreed on:

(1) a position,
(2) a tactic,
(3) doing it.

This seems simple, but for women it means that formidable psychological hurdles have been overcome. Anytime you see a group of women taking an action in behalf of humanity—applaud.

Strike a Balance

Because these elements—concern, self-study, spreading the word, service, organization, action—are presented serially doesn't mean they have to occur in that order, or that as we move from one to the other, we need drop the others. As a matter of fact, the best organizations include all of these elements, and try to strike some kind of fluctuating balance. An action that is hot demands major attention, and service projects or study are neglected. But when action is stalled for a while—waiting for a particular bill to come out of committee, for example—those same projects are very useful to keep the membership involved and happy. Service projects can be a step toward organization and action, too.

Also, people join a group at different stages of political need. Some want to be educated, some want a base from which to speak out, some are anxious to get moving. Rather than make everyone conform to one single-minded purpose, flexible organizations utilize these varied interests to make committees work.

There is no one way to function; all elements should be considered. Too much "education" without action is unproductive. All action without concern for ideas becomes thoughtless and automatic. No service, at least to the membership, takes away the human quality, but all service diverts it from social change. Organization for its own sake without the other elements is the most deadly of all.

We Band Together for Power

To women, power is a frightening word, but it need not be. Power should be: having a say in things that affect our lives; representing truly or being truly represented; influencing decisions; being listened to and respected; becoming a full person with others who are likewise full people. Power should not be: a "trip"; oppressing others; assuming superiority; making unilateral decisions; not listening or respecting others; ceasing to struggle for the personhood of all.

An idealist view of power? Of course, but that's what activism is about—moving the world toward an ideal.

Criteria for Selecting an Organization

In choosing an ongoing group in which to be active, strip away the window dressing and look at the organization with a cool eye. Consider who belongs and why. Note who does the work (if they do any) and what has been accomplished—potential as well as immediate programs. Be sure to give special attention to women's role if it is a mixed group. Here are some questions to keep in mind:

What are the organization's stated aims? These are usually couched in general terms to allow flexibility in program, or to encourage a wide spectrum of support. But unless the association at least *says* it's what you are for, you won't have much room to function.

What does it do about these aims? Specifically: Educate the public? Take stands? Work in coalition? Act? Especially, what does it do on the more controversial part of its program? The gap between theory and practice is sometimes enormous.

How much time is spent in housekeeping? Like houses, organizations that demand constant upkeep can be more trouble than they're worth. Consider how much time and effort is spent in financing, maintenance, and unproductive chores just to keep the organization alive. Women's groups are especially suspectible to this failing.

What would be my role? First, decide what you want. If you would rather just pay dues, receive a newsletter, and perhaps fill out a ballot once a year, that's one thing. Supportive membership serves a purpose, particularly when your special interests are elsewhere. But if you are looking for active involvement, that's something else. Check how many women are on the board of directors, on the staff, and in responsible positions. Ask questions.

What would it do for me? An organization should give as well as receive. Ask yourself: What could I learn? Will it be stimulating? Creative? Move me along toward my goals? (Men don't join the Rotary just out of benevolence.)

How about the social aspects? People band together as much from social needs as from desire to affect society. Since one way to overcome alienation is working together on commonly felt issues, a group of people who can accomplish this feels a sense of community. The longer and harder the battle, the deeper the friendships grow. Recognize that instant relationships seldom happen, so judge the social potential of a group after participating fully over a period of time. Some organizations fill a special social need: opportunity for a husband and wife to work on something together; a chance for a single woman to meet persons of the opposite sex in a positive setting; a place for a newcomer to make friends; freedom for a woman to work with other women without male domination. All are valid group functions.

What could I contribute? Saved for last, because we're usually too selfless, this is still an essential question. There's no pleasure in it if you can't contribute, and the more you do, the more satisfaction. Perhaps you can help a timid organization act on its stated aims. Maybe you have the spark that was lacking. Forget the modesty and admit, "They *need* me."

It's a good idea to shop around for a while before deciding where you belong. You will be investing some time and money; make it a careful selection, not just a happening.

Or, Form Your Own

§ A group of neighbors, talking over coffee, are incensed about the third rise in the price of bread. They decide to protest. Excited by their own boldness, they make picket signs, draw up a leaflet, and appear at the supermarket. Many shoppers stop to talk to them. They find the unaccustomed defiance so exhilarating that they meet again to form a consumer organization.

§ Renters in a housing complex sit around someone's living room. They introduce themselves and tell about their housing difficulties: inadequate heating, broken plumbing, unsafe porches. "I have that same problem" is frequently heard. A list of grievances is drawn up and presented to the landlord, who predictably refuses to deal with them as a group—at first. Over a period of time, as a tenant's union, they learn to cope with the complex legal maze they are up against, and at the same time develop close ties as neighbors and friends.

§ Family members of prisoners, angry and frustrated with the penal system, band together to give support to each other and to prisoners. Together they find ways to function as an information service and to publicize those issues that they feel are repressive.

All the above are action groups formed by the persons most directly involved. They vary in how they operate, because in organization, *form follows function*. Here are more examples:

§ In a small community, where trucks regularly passed through a populated area without a stop sign, a child was run over and killed. Outraged mothers formed a human gate, refusing to let the trucks go by. The matter went to court and was settled by conciliation, but not before a community organization was formed to fight for the parents' interests. In this case a spontaneous expression of outrage in response to crisis led to organization.

§ Small groups of divorced women are getting together in various cities for mutual support and also for practical help. They usually include women who have "been through it all" and can give advice on credit problems, employment, and the many little things that harass a newly separated woman who has been long dependent upon a man. Loneliness is a major concern, so they go places together and are available to each other in time of crisis or depression. They may also be engaged in legislative reforms, such as liberalization of divorce laws. This is a mutual-aid group based upon common needs and problems.

§ *Consumer Action Now* (CAN) is an environmental source for the consumer. Twenty unpaid but committed women produce a well-documented newsletter with the emphasis on "conserve" rather than "consume." The main objective is to relate the consumer to the environment. As a result of the newsletter, CAN members have been in demand for speaking engagements, interviews, and testimony at hearings, both locally and in Washington. In one year circulation has grown to six thousand in all the states and five other countries. *If we have to live here,* they said, *we'll make it livable.*

§ "Only a woman who has been through it can help another," said Mae Rose Shelton, coordinator of Chicago's Woodlawn Sisterhood of welfare mothers. Ms. Shelton divides the mothers into the weak (who need help) and the strong (who are in a position to help). "An outsider does not function well." She describes the terrible depression, so great that a woman may not be able to cook a meal for her hungry children. "The only personal contact this woman may have is with a male friend who comes by once a month to help her spend her welfare check on alcohol." The women developed a program to help the "weak" sisters. When such a woman is discovered, a sister wins her confidence and involves her "within the loving environment of the sisterhood." "It is said that a black woman can make a way out of no way." The Woodlawn Sisterhood is working on the ways.

§ *The Berkeley Women's Health Collective* is a medically oriented group. They run a weekly free clinic in the basement of a church. Trained nonprofessionals working in conjunction with physicians and nurses offer personalized treatment. Many of the women are active in the Medical Committee for Human Rights, and are bent on the radical politicalization of medicine. As one woman medic put it, "We believe that health care for women by women will prove to be one of the most permanent, viable things to come out of the Women's Movement." The collective is creating an alternative institutional structure, composed of clinic and women's small groups.

§ *Consumer's Medical Association* is a national group of women who started in the abortion reform movement two years ago. Their aim is to improve doctor-patient communications in all areas of medicine, but they are especially interested in self-pelvic examinations including do-it-yourself pregnancy tests. "Pap smear kits have been available to women in Canada for years, so why not here?" asked Merle Goldberg of the Association. The group is out to destroy the "medical mystique" and break through the medical price structure, she states. The CMA has 50 chapters across the country, and works through existing self-help clinics, health bureaus and abortion groups to *educate the health consumer.*

Whatever the purpose of the association, the organizational form should reflect it. The function may change, but so then will the form. For example, the housewives who boycotted paid major attention to action: picketing the supermarket. They channeled energy into writing leaflets, making picket signs, confronting the manager, and talking to shoppers. Later, as the group became a consumer organization, they paid more attention to building membership, finance, and committees. But since holding down prices is the basic intent of the organization, actions to accomplish that purpose must continue, or the organization will die.

The clearer the group is on its function, the better it can answer its organizational questions.

Here are some typical questions that come up:

• *Should we form a chapter of an existing national body, or create something new?* The answer depends on how loose you want to hang; whether you want to affect national policy—if there is an organization you feel is right on.

• *How many officers should we have?* Elections can kill or cure. Sometimes they function like a traffic light turning green. When elected, the person standing on the curb sees the signal change from DON'T WALK to WALK, and starts to run.

• *Who needs a hierarchy?* If ego-tripping seems to be the main danger, keep organization loose and in the hands of the membership. *Good* leadership can galvanize a group and be a catalyst for everybody's growth.

• *Should we incorporate?* If you need tax deductibility, you have to. You may also want to protect yourselves from personal liability. Discuss it with a lawyer.

• *Should we have committees?* Committees are great if they function. If not, they become resting places for good intentions.

• *How often should we meet?* Any organization worth its salt has at least a nucleus that gives considerable time. Not wanting to meet is a symptom of organizational fatigue.

• *How can I get people motivated?* The leader who complains about her troops should first look to her own leadership.

Just because it is made up of people, no group can avoid all the miseries. Organization is always a battle to move forward under the incredible odds of apathy, timidity, discouragement, shattered illusions, and hostilities.

Organizing is hell. So what else is new?

The Question of Style

Have you ever gone to a meeting and said, "What am I doing here?" Was it because . . .

• You felt like an outsider? Nobody seemed to care that you had made the effort to come?

• They talked about things you couldn't follow because they didn't bother to explain technicalities?

• They discussed trivialities and accomplished nothing? They didn't seem to mind wasting their time, but you did?

• You didn't want to get involved in *that* kind of action?

• They just weren't your kind of people?

• They bickered so much that you felt uncomfortable and left out?

• You could see they would put demands on you that you were not willing to accept?

• They didn't seem to know what they were doing?

• They were so well-informed that you felt like a fool, and if you stayed with the group, they would soon find you out?

• You could see the action they were planning wouldn't get anywhere—or would backfire?

It might not seem so on the surface, but all these reactions are in part related to the question of style. Birds of a feather usually join the same organization.

Class and cultural differences

Try attending a meeting of a welfare-rights group, an action-oriented student group, a middle-class-housewives' organization, a feminist women's small group, a brown or black organization, a business and professional women's association. Although there will be issues in common, you may feel you are visiting different countries. Class and cultural differences very much affect the language we use (including what we consider obscenities), the way we dress, how the meeting is run, the type of action considered appropriate, and how individuals act toward each other. Accepting differences of style along with similarities of cause makes coalition possible.

Age differences

Young women in a consciousness-raising group are at an opposite pole from the League of Women Voters when it comes to style, but eventually their common sex will prove an essential link. Because there has been a revulsion of young people against the "hypocrisy, ineffectiveness, and conformity" of their elders, they reject the old way of doing things and struggle to create new forms. Recognizing these dissimilarities—and the reasons for them—helps to reach across the age barrier. (Of course, the stretch has to be two-way.)

Sex differences

"I just can't stand to work in women's groups!" Why do so many of us feel like that? Perhaps it is because our old organizations reflect the pseudoworld in which we functioned. Nothing stands still, however, and the most conservative organizations are awakening to the new wave of feminism, while deploring "its methods."

"I can't work with men in the group" is the other side of the coin. Not necessarily man-haters, some feminists feel that women defer to men in a mixed organization. Because of this deference—and because men expect to lead—males tend to take over leadership, and women are hesitant to speak freely when men are present.

The new sisterhood is uniting with high hopes and wildly divergent aims. If most of what goes on in its name doesn't seem very sisterly, well, neither are blood sisters from time to time.

Interpersonal relations

If you feel put down at a meeting, or just plain ignored, you may react by:

—determining that you will stick it out until you are finally accepted for what you can contribute . . .

—deciding that the organization doesn't know what it is doing, so you will drop out . . .

—deciding to give them another chance and if it happens again, that's it . . .

—concluding that they must be right and that you have nothing to offer anyway, so why waste your time and theirs?

How do *you* react?

Some groups go out of their way to make people feel comfortable—and wanted. Others—generally those based on male models—are too caught up with the business at hand to take the time for "sensitivity." The most successful action groups usually strike a balance. On the one hand, they try to be open and accepting. On the other, they avoid the therapy trap.

How things are run

In a formal structure where Robert's Rules are king, you had better study up on that handbook and come in fighting. The purpose of such formalism is to achieve democracy, and a good case can be made that, properly applied, it does. But the uninitiated find themselves at a great disadvantage.

At the other end of the range are the consensus-minded. A real consensus is more than getting everyone to agree to something. Groups trying to set up alternative structures are attempting to share not only decision-making, but carrying out of decisions as well. The women's health collective, described earlier, even tries to share technical skills. Members are committed to competence in all the work they do.

More commonly there is the leadership and the "others" (usually referred to as the membership). The knowledgeable few run things, while anyone else is expected to work her or his way into the inner circle by virtue of seniority or hard work. Most of the doers would be delighted to welcome others into their circle to share the burdens, but often they are ineffective in opening the door. As a rule, women need an inordinate amount of reassurance before we can make that leap.

What action should be taken?

Style differences often boil down to degree of militancy. Most established organizations of women are not likely to want to rock the boat. Reforms are to be accomplished through proper channels. Most congenial would be a statement to the press, testimony at a hearing, or a letter to an appropriate body. Above all, a "ladylike" style must be maintained. Even limited action on an accepted principle may have to overcome hurdles of a board of trustees, fearful of controversy. Style is part of the image the organization sets for itself, which might be tarnished by an ill-advised act.

Partisan political action has its own style

A new feminist political style is emerging behind candidates like Bella Abzug of New York. Brash, vigorous, and enthusiastic, it is flourishing as women's political caucuses are forming in each community. Activist energies will break through old barriers of what we can or cannot do, and will probably affect the style of women activists across the board.

The new Portias

Since 1964, when sex discrimination was "outlawed" by the Civil Rights Act, there has been an increasing amount of legal action by women. A brand-new style has emerged. Classes on "women and the law," feminist law practices and collectives, and a surge of female applicants to law schools are much in evidence. Women's civil rights organizations such as the National Organization for Women and Women's Equity Action League (WEAL) are carrying the struggle into the courtroom. This hitherto all-male arena has been invaded by women, and, once initiated into its mysteries, we'll not turn back. Since women recognize that *institutions* must be changed to get at our problems, we are becoming law-minded. Expect more female legal activists, and these will not be limited to attorneys by any means.

No group can be moved into a style too far removed from its own experience . . . just a short step at a time. Once having experienced street distribution of leaflets, for example, a group might consider carrying a sign—*if* enough others are doing likewise. Organizers attempt to start from the style most comfortable to the group involved, and work toward whatever tactic will bring results.

Blasting Off

To anyone new to organization, getting a new group off the ground may seem a formidable task, but it's not that hard if the issues appeal. Women are organizable, and growing more so daily. There are three basic steps:

(1) An organizing nucleus—three or more dedicated persons willing to work their tails off.

(2) Publicity (getting the word out to potential members).

(3) A public meeting (or meetings).

Around these steps there can be innumerable variations, depending on purpose, constituency, and style. The publicity could be a standard press release or a show-stopper; the meeting may be formal or a happening. But it's worth putting real effort into the blast-off. Dare to be bold. A timid start will take time to overcome, while real impact in the beginning will speed things along.

For example, immediately following the tragic death of Martin Luther King, Jr., a handful of women in Los Angeles decided that positive moves by whites were desperately needed. They wrote the "Join Hands Pledge," an action-oriented statement of principles opposed to racism. Then they gathered their friends around and circulated that pledge widely for signatures, collecting money for a newspaper ad from each signer. Within the incredibly brief period of two weeks they had gathered over a thousand signatures, which were included with the pledge in a huge display ad in the Los Angeles *Times*. These women caught the crest of public concern for injustice to blacks in white America. From this auspicious start they proceeded to organize one of the few viable white action groups on the problem of racism.

Not all organizations can start with such a splash. Take the Kitsap County, Washington, chapter of NOW. A handful of women in this semi-rural area decided a feminist group was needed in their community. They were the organizing nucleus, or "conveners," as they are called in NOW terminology. At their planning meeting each person prepared a personal mailing list from organizations she belonged to. Invitational letters were sent to presidents of all women's organizations (list from Chambers of Commerce). Conveners who belonged to any group enclosed a personal note.

"Our first open meeting was rather formal (maybe too formal), but we kept in mind that we had in attendance a fair number of club presidents and other community leaders who were probably *not* interested in becoming members but who most definitely *were* interested in finding out how 'Women's Libbers' looked and behaved." Kitsap County NOW got off to a good solid start, an organizational model for others in small towns and rural areas.

15.
FINDING TEAMMATES

Rights are never given. They are real only when they are fought for and won. Over and over again, unfortunately. If this is so, people are the end and not the means. What a miserable long-range viewpoint!

But it's the only way to answer that nagging question, "But what did you really accomplish? You got the bill passed, but nothing has basically changed." Something *has* changed. Everyone who worked on that campaign

(1) has decided you can't beat the establishment so you had better join it.

(2) has become disillusioned and is retiring from the Movement.

(3) is already mapping out the next steps.

When the "Who?" question is given its proper weight, more of us will choose that third alternative.

Finding teammates is central to any campaign. The image of a team has salesman connotations, but it's better than the usual military terms (corps, task force, troop, company), because a team is more of an ensemble and less of a hierarchy. Neither our language nor our society provides good images of a real working collective. At any rate, a team feeling has to develop to get a movement going—"our side"—an esprit de corps, to fall back on the military. Black consciousness, *la raza,* and sisterhood are examples. Since most underdogs have been trained to despise themselves, a conscious development of pride is an essential element.

Women as change agents

If women are to become more active, we will undergo both subtle and spectacular changes. To some, these transformations will appear as "unfeminine." Curiously, assertiveness, self-confidence, assurance, and articulateness are seldom seen as unfeminine unless they are displayed in a wave-making situation. But when we use all our resources in the realm where the real decisions are made, especially in the service of an unpopular cause (like our own), the femininity question will be raised against us, and we should be prepared to face it. The more success an agent for change has, the more vulnerable she or he becomes. The only real defense of the individual lies within the group, which is a major reason for organizing in the first place.

Teaming Techniques

Like tactics, a whole variety of techniques to recruit, to cultivate and to involve new teammates moves the action forward:

Keep a people record. For example, when someone calls with a question, record the name, address, and phone, the subject, and what you did about it. Keep this in a 3″x5″-card box, or in a journal. Add names from all your other contacts, but note something about each person to jog your memory. If you have occasion to call her, you have a starting point. "How are you feeling now? You were just out of the hospital the last time I spoke to you," or "Did that bill go through that you were working on?" Also keep a file of letters to the editor on issues that interest you, together with news clippings mentioning persons working in these fields. Collect lists of names from organizations and committees.

Talent scout. Big-time sports promoters build their teams this way, and so can we. Don't waste your time on *any* meeting, class, lecture, or other gathering without coming away with at least one name (plus address and phone) for present or future activity. Also look for speakers and panelists. Sample record:

> Joan Takaki spoke 11–2–71 at Women's Peace Coalition Workshop. Subject: an alternative budget for peace. Good, especially in question and answer period. Asst. professor in poly. sci. at State college. Spoke to her afterward. Might be available to speak after exams next month. Call after ——.

Across a crowded room. Suppose you are in a meeting called to consider a social issue. Most of the women are strangers, but as the discussion goes along a few express positions that are similar to yours. When the coffee break comes, don't waste time with those you talked to yesterday; make a beeline for the beautiful strangers. Express agreement, if you have not already done so publicly, and exchange names. Find out what you can of their organizational and work ties, and what activities they are currently involved in. Record.

New blood. Publishers know that every new subscription is worth more than a renewal. Although a fresh recruit to activism is a jewel, unfortunately many organizations set up psychological obstacles to participation without being aware of it. On any issue there are people waiting on the sidelines, wishing they had the courage to dive in, in need only of a gentle shove. An organizer has her antenna out and encourages the first timid sign of interest. Neighbors, friends, classmates, or even casual acquaintances may join if they are continually invited to do so *and* not pushed too fast.

Nurturing. Most women new to activism need assistance. Take plenty of time to explain things, to answer questions, and to help the newcomer get started. A woman who has confined herself to domestic problems may be an excellent organizer in that realm, but feel woefully inadequate at a meeting where people speak in legislative jargon. She is not likely to volunteer for a committee, thinking that she has nothing to bring to it. An invitation might be, "Will you help me with . . ." In working together, especially on a one-to-one basis, the oldtimer can:

(1) provide the newcomer with all the background information necessary, including written materials, and

(2) discover her strong points and special interests so that she can be plugged into the organization where she is able both to contribute and to learn the most.

Good parenting equals good human relations. Give no more help than necessary, but lots of support. The time should soon come to say, "You're doing it so well now, would you take the responsibility and we'll find someone to help *you?*" The careful nurturing of a new activist will reap a double harvest. She will first of all become a useful participant in the action at hand, but also, like a parent who rears a child as she was reared, she will probably treat other new members in the same manner as she was treated. There is no other explanation for the sink-or-swim way many organizations treat new participants than that the members survived the same method and expect others to do as well. ("I pulled myself out of poverty. Why can't they?")

Therapy. There is more than education involved, especially in female groups. Ego massage is as vital to an action as a good leaflet. Second-class citizenship has left its scars, and these need to be recognized and dealt with in a supportive way. Besides encouraging the timid, there are the little ego trips to deal with. Be patient.

Matchmaking. Bring people together. "You know Joan Takaki at State College? She's very interested in that question. Perhaps you and she could work something up for the conference. Here is her number. I'll call her too, and give her yours." Then do so: "Joan Takaki? I heard you speak at the Women's Peace Coalition workshop. A friend of mine, Jane Kaplan, has been working along the same lines as you. We wondered if you would be interested in helping her with a statement for . . . ?" Most new friends thank their matchmakers, making allowances for the occasional error in judgment that is inevitable.

Trade-offs. For the old-timers a different approach is needed. Persons already into action probably have a project or two of their own to push. No matter how interested they are in your cause, it will be more inviting if they can at the same time further their own projects. Busy activists usually have several balls in the air at one time and are not going to set aside prior obligations entirely. If they can see ways of integrating the issues or new opportunities to present their ongoing commitments, they will be more receptive. "Would you work with us on this conference? I realize how busy you are, especially with the prison-reform bill. If you would like to set up a table with materials on that subject at the conference, there will be room in the lobby."

Work parties. In all volunteer organizations there are considerable quantities of drudge work, some of which can be turned into socializing situations. Even when it is easier to do it yourself than to organize a group to do a mailing, for example, a work party provides an opportunity for the newcomer to take part on an equal level with everyone else. For example, the New York chapter of NOW planned a fund-raising party. At a membership meeting, "we asked that anyone interested in helping address envelopes or donate food sign their names and phone numbers on a sheet we sent around. Out of the twenty-seven who signed, we got about twelve active workers. We talked with them while we addressed envelopes (almost all of them were new members). We discovered that among these new members were people with experience in putting on large parties. We asked several to help with the planning. Each of these people was given a specific project." Committee members were secured, the party raised $1,400, and, best of all, new activists from the fringes joined the magic circle.

How to Hold a Public Meeting

When you want to bring the community into the act, one way is to line up a good speaker, publicize the event well, notify any other groups who might be interested, have a good discussion, talk to people (as individuals), and follow up.

Organizational Outline

I. "Mailing Party." Invite anyone who will come, and especially new members, but without pressure. Ask everyone to bring current lists, unless you already have sufficient names.
   A. Have ready materials to be mailed (e.g. leaflets, cover letters, envelopes), mailing list on cards, stamp pads, stamps.
   B. When finished, go over outline and make assignments.
   C. Discuss additional personal contacts people have, especially friends who belong to organizations.

II. Publicity
   A. Make list of newspapers and TV and radio station in area.
   B. Write basic press release. Secure photo of speaker if possible.
   C. Call newspersons (e.g. woman's editor) as soon as date is set. Deliver photo and release in person if possible. At least a follow-up call. Allow plenty of time.

   D. List special types of publicity: church bulletins? organization newsletters? advertising press?

III. Your organization meeting
   A. Sell the coming event to the membership.
   B. Have extra leaflets available, and extra letters.
   C. Ask everyone to go through personal phone books and call at least 5 people.
   D. Who knows who? Have a list of all the groups or people you want personally notified of the event. As you run down the list, pin down responsibility.

IV The Meeting. Make it run smoothly. Organization women are as critical of sloppy organization as others are of poor housekeeping. Set up tables for "donation" and literature as needed.
   A. Speakers' table (e.g., chair-one, person to introduce speaker, speaker). Guest book: names, addresses, zip codes for mailing list.
   B. Start no more than 15 minutes late.
   C. Additional table for coffee, tea, and maybe cookies. (We women usually eat at our meetings.) Plenty of ashtrays.
   D. Membership: if this is your purpose, have plenty of materials, applications, and pens available, and at least 2 persons to concentrate on this. Some newcomers will want to think about it. Be sure they have address to mail application and check, and number to call. Next meeting should be carefully announced. A brief presentation on your organization will help.

Don't ask, is it worth it? Each contact made, list compiled, task learned can be used again. The first time is a lot of work; next time will be like rolling off a log.

Our Woman in City Hall (Cultivating the Grass Roots)

Suppose you have organized, mobilized, registered, educated, got out the vote, and at last *elected* a spokeswoman * to the city

* Or, of course, "spokesperson" or "spokes one."

council. You are no longer "the silenced majority" because you have a *voice* where policies are made.

But there she sits—lonely, exposed, vulnerable—the only woman in a masculine arena. Although deferred to and treated politely, she is not listened to. Nor is she taken seriously by other council members and city officials—because she is female, a beginner, and has been elected by Outsiders. The powers that be have no handle on her. All they can do is ignore her and hope she will go away next election.

What do you do? (Choose one.)

(1) You worked hard to elect her. Now it's up to her to produce.

(2) She's helpless. That shows you that there's no use messing with politics!

(3) Build a support team—both as pressure group and as preparation for the next stage: a power bloc.

The third alternative requires as much work as it did to put her in office, without election fever to kindle enthusiasm. But anything that has to be done can be done. If women are to play a significant role in political life, there is no other way.

A *starting point* is the campaign machinery, which had to be good to get her elected in the first place. There must be at least one skilled organizer, lots of names, and telephoners.

Quite naturally, there is a tendency after an election to give major attention to the office with all its new problems. Learning the ropes, making contacts, just becoming acquainted with the job are themselves formidable tasks. But it might be better to slow down the orientation program in order to consolidate the grass roots. A new politician will not accomplish much at first anyway, and will be able to move much faster with troops beside her.

Possible forms (in which to apply all the teaming techniques mentioned above, combined with ingenuity and drive):

§ *Visible support.* Make every council meeting "Woman's Night at the Council." Make a *thing* of it. A "tour guide" or hostess should be present to explain what is going on, answer questions, and provide brief hand-outs summarizing the business at hand (with necessary glossary for councilese) and the councilwoman's

viewpoint or questions on matters on which she wants input. Her "logo" should be displayed on everything, including the guide. Encourage registration, with room to answer: I am especially interested in ____.
All such names should be added to the "people" record. All women's organizations should be invited to attend, as groups if possible. ("An invitation from your councilwoman to participate in city government . . .") When issues of special concern come up for discussion, put the telephone and publicity forces to work on packing the house. There is no better way to give support to your councilwoman than physical presence. When an audience is listening, officials will have to listen to her too.

§ *Invisible support.* Berkeley Councilwoman Ilona Hancock has a weekly work session with volunteer supporters in which the packet of council matters to come before the body at the next meeting are reviewed, discussed, and assigned for additional study. This not only helps her, but is an excellent training ground in political activism. There should be a talent bank: a pool of people to draw on for opinions, research, statements, and organizational tasks. Attention to nurturing and talent-scouting will pay off well. A skilled communications person would be invaluable.

§ *Media involvement.* A careful search for teammates on radio or TV may open opportunities for a "report to my constituency" on a regular basis. Two-way communication, which helps build the "we" feeling, might be improved by an "open telephone" radio show. Continually invite women to participate, at council meetings, at the open caucus, and by mail.

§ *Open meeting.* Once a month conduct an informal meeting in a school or other public place to discuss issues and problems as candidly as possible. The atmosphere should be friendly and easy, with no gulf between the politician and her constituents. Goals are education (both ways), recruiting new blood, and building solidarity. If the same excitement that was generated to get the candidate elected can be turned into helping her run the city, the impact could be enormous. When time permits (she will be tired by now), the councilwoman should speak before women's organizations in the same manner.

§ *Membership and funds.* Some structure, loose as it may be, should eventually jell, perhaps out of the open meeting. (We are talking about organization independent of political party structure, on the assumption that this office is nonpartisan.) For its purpose, the more fluid the structure, the better, so long as it can involve people and raise money. Unfortunately, fund raising cannot stop when the campaign expenses are paid for.

§ *Past, present, and future.* Difficult to do under pressure, but all three tenses must be kept in mind:

(1) Remember who elected her—keep the fences mended.

(2) Meet current issues as well as possible. That's very relative, and "priority" is the key word here.

. . . *Guess it's time for a caucus.*

(3) Lay the basis for a team inside city hall. This includes alliances, as well as appointments to commissions, staff, and special bodies. She will know who can do what.

Politicians get lost in problems of time. They are either overly concerned with paying off their political debts or have their eye on the next election. Women's candidates must be rooted in the past, coping with the present, and taking an active part in shaping the future. No one woman can do all that without standing on the shoulders of many more. Never underestimate the power of a team of women.

16.
THE CAUCUS

If it's *your* organization—you helped to form it, and it's made up of people more or less of like mind—you have one set of problems. Suppose you belong to an association, however, where you are an Outsider. You may be in the minority because of sex or race or viewpoint. There's not much you can accomplish, and you may stop attending meetings, or decide to drop out. That is where the caucus comes in.

A large number of professional organizations now have black, Chicano, and women's caucuses to fight for representation and changes in policy. Radical caucuses are shaking even the staidest of associations. For women the caucus form has tremendous potential:

• Women gain courage when they tackle the male powers that be as a unit.

• Men become defensive when confronted by a block of earnest or angry women. They are used to dealing with females one by one and are skilled at doing so. But they are quite taken aback by a group of us.

• There is no quicker way to form a team. The spirit of "our side" makes it more difficult for fence-sitters to defect.

• Experiencing a taste of power can embolden new activists to heights they never knew they could attempt.

• If women play their hands well (ask for more than they expect, divide the opposition, build their demands on stated principles), they will probably come out with not only representation, but opportunity to shift the direction in which the body is moving.

A fine case study of a woman's caucus can be found in the annals of the Modern Language Association. This professional organization is comprised of college-level teachers of language and literature. Like other such prestigious bodies, the MLA was in effect a male club. Eight women had served on the Executive Council in all its seventy-eight years.

At the 1968 convention, a woman's caucus made its appearance, throwing the leadership off balance, and resulting in passage of several feminist resolutions. One of them charged the Executive Council with appointing a commission to investigate the status of women in the profession, and to make recommendations with regard to establishing "equity." The commission was to report annually to the convention.

During the following year, all hell broke loose. Suits * charging sex discrimination were filed against some two hundred colleges and universities, mostly by the Women's Equity Action League (WEAL). Of these suits, fifty or more were referrals from the MLA Commission, the result of letters pouring into that office from unhappy women on campuses all over the country.

Meanwhile the commission itself was having its consciousness raised. "Ours is in large part a *woman's* profession, yet on the higher levels of the profession we are poorly represented," they stated. These were no idle charges. Homework had been carefully prepared by experts in how to make assignments.

Back on the campus, conditions had not changed that much. MLA females were now in that painful situation of a high level of consciousness and too little progress. Furthermore, the bottom was dropping out of the college teaching job market. The demands had escalated, reflecting heightened participation. The crunch will come when female consciousness meets job shortages.

What's to be learned from the MLA women?

* The legal basis for the action is contract compliance, or Executive Order No. 11375, prohibiting discrimination by government contractors. Over 80 percent of U.S. colleges are subject to this order, according to the U.S. Department of Health, Education and Welfare (HEW).

. . . A caucus is a recognition of a common cause, an effort to organize a team, make demands, push for representation. It is the Outsider's way of demanding a voice.

. . . The caucus was effective because *the participants did not go home and forget about it.*

. . . A spectrum of tactics was used, within the style of the membership for the most part, but experimenting with new forms. The most significant new effort was the compliance suit.

. . . Reports were scholarly and well-researched without losing urgency. "Gentlemen's agreements" were exposed.

. . . In keeping with sharpened consciousness, demands escalated and became more specific.

. . . The MLA caucus is part of a movement, and draws sustenance from outside the ivy halls.

Caucuses work especially well in professional organizations, but are not limited to these. The newest area is in institutionalized religions. Here women have had considerable grass-roots organizational experience, and are beginning to put it to use in new directions. For example, the churchwomen's caucus of the United Methodist Church called a national meeting to get it together in preparation for the church's General Conference, spring of 1972. "Issues of concurrence" were (1) women in every decision-making body of the church in proportion to membership (and in leadership positions), and (2) a commission on women to continue to deal with issues related to sexism in the church. The meeting gave special attention to church structure, desired changes and to tactics. The caucus was *organizing.*

MEN—MOVE OVER.

17.
MEETINGS AND THEIR HANG-UPS

A meeting is a social contract. We attend a meeting for:

. . . mutual aid, because we need to band together to get something done.

. . . recognition from each other.

. . . reinforcement ("I'm not alone in my concern").

If anything happens—and that is not always the case—the meeting becomes more than the sum of the people who attend. A new entity is formed: a collective.

We also attend a meeting to play games, in the Eric-Berne-*Games-People-Play* sense. Most of these interfere with the social contract that brought us into the group in the first place, though we derive some satisfaction from them (or stop attending). From the organizational point of view, these games are hang-ups that prevent the contract from being fulfilled. They are often the reason for the common response "Of course I think it's important, but I just can't stand meetings." Because they are satisfying to some, games are hard to overcome, but they can be minimized or bypassed. Once recognized, one can at least avoid becoming an unwilling player. Here are some common ones:

"Meeting to Beget Meetings." This is literally a pastime, and is common among women starved for meaning in their lives. After the first feminist wave, reform energies of women were siphoned into a pseudoworld of clubs and organizations, functioning on the fringe of the "real" world. Meetings became an end in themselves: "If we have to meet about it, our project must be worthwhile." The more meetings, the more valuable the activity.

"Fill the Time Available." Because they are unpaid, many women place little value on their time. The number of hours to accomplish a task is not considered, in the same way that housework is often performed to fill the time, rather than to accomplish a specific purpose. The project may be more a pastime than an end in itself, as in numerous fund-raising activities that raise little money but keep the members busy for weeks.

"Ain't It Awful?" This is a hard game to avoid in groups concerned with social change, because what *is* awful has to be explored before there is enough concern or knowledge to do anything about it. But when discussion goes on endlessly—beware. Games are in progress. You will hear how brainwashed (racist/sexist/backward/materialistic/sheeplike/selfish/stupid) *they* are. The game is revealed when action is suggested.

"Why Don't You . . . Yes, But . . ." Another Berne game, very popular in female groups, goes something like this:

An "expert" has been invited to a meeting. A question-and-answer period follows until someone asks the inevitable "What can we do?"

EXPERT: Why don't you write to . . .
MEMBER: Yes, we did that but they didn't answer . . .
EXPERT: Well, why not send a delegation to talk . . .

MEMBER: They would just refer us back to . . .

EXPERT: Why don't you have some speakers who could go out to other groups and see if you can get more support . . .

MEMBER: People just don't care enough about it in those groups . . .

EXPERT: Well, you might try a petition . . .

MEMBER: Yes, but we couldn't get enough people to carry them to make it worthwhile.

Silence. The speaker knows the game is lost. The members feel quite satisfied with themselves, having proved that they have considered every angle, and that indeed it would be fruitless to do anything more.

"Numbers." One version is another form of "Ain't It Awful?" The moment of truth comes when an action is to be taken and someone points out that "there are not enough of us to *do* anything." This is followed by an arsenal of reasons why nothing could possibly be accomplished, given the small number of committed persons (us) who really care. Another version is "Body Count." Success is measured only in terms of attendance. "Did you have a successful meeting?" "Yes, thirty people came." "What did you decide on?" "They're all going to ask someone else to come next time." This often leads to "Taking in Each Other's Laundry." Each chair one attends the others' meeting to make it a "success," until everyone is so busy that nothing is carried through.

"Smorgasbord" is a favorite game of women who want to be "involved" but avoid responsibility. In order to become "informed" the person flits from cause to cause, interested in everything—to a point. Playing it loose may be a good way to begin, but, continued too long, ends up as dilettantism.

"Horseshoe Nail" is another version played by very active groups. An elaborate plan is worked out and preparations get under way, but a small but vital part of the plan is neglected—such as a telephone call to the key speaker. Since there wasn't much confidence that the plan would come off anyway, the whole thing collapses like a pack of cards. Participants are inwardly relieved.

When a few members of a group really do get into high gear, they often end up **"Overloading the Circuits."** This may be a game, done to prove how impossible it is for a woman to carry out community action. She may take on one responsibility after another until finally she blows a fuse. Then she throws down everything and isn't heard from again. Dr. Berne, who describes a similar housewife game he calls "Harried," explains it on the basis of that great favorite of psychiatrists: penis envy. In my experience, most women who take on too much do so from inability to say no, a sense of urgency, or a first awakening to a more rewarding lifestyle. Eventually they learn to pace themselves, or take occasional breaks. The best recourse is to adopt the rhythm method (for organization only): Modulate intense periods by periods of relative calm.

Most meetings are like a marriage gone stale. Nothing unexpected happens: members accept each other or don't, bicker or are generally polite, and settle down to a routine with everyone in familiar roles. Instead, we should strive to make meetings more like love affairs, filled with excitement and suspense. They should lead to commitment—even overcommitment. Members should experience an emotional heightening and feeling of being alive. Not at all times perhaps, for even the best affair has its quiet moments. Ah, those are the meetings to remember!

Meeting Analysis

Attending a meeting should not be a spectator sport. Whether you are in the chair or a newcomer, the social contract covers everyone present. Responsibility may be heaviest on the persons up front, but in order to build a collective all members have to feel responsible. Keep these questions in mind when a strategy is under discussion.

(1) What is the issue before us?
(2) What are we *ready, willing,* and *able* to do about it?
(3) What alternatives have been presented?
(4) What are the areas of agreement? Disagreement?
(5) What is the first step?

Analytical thinking helps to see the whole picture without getting lost in personalities and word games. When you are concentrating in this active manner while listening to what is going on, you can usually come through with some constructive ideas to move the group forward. Try it at the next meeting you attend.

One Dozen Cage-Breakers for Meetings

(1) *Try the ready-willing-and-able formula* on any proposed project. Is the group *ready* (prepared, convinced) to move on this? Are the members *willing* to do what is required? Are they *able* to carry it through to a satisfactory conclusion?

(2) *Break up the games.* Pin "Ain't It Awful?" players down, even at the risk of losing some. Be prepared with back-up for the "Horseshoe Nail" type who forgets the crucial call. Insist that every meeting lead somewhere. Be conscious of someone "Overloading the Circuits," and help her unload something.

(3) *Experiment with new forms of meeting.* If it is too structured, try passing the leadership around. If there are no leaders, try selecting someone to be expeditor or catalyst.

(4) *Know who comes and why.* If the meeting isn't too large, you can start out by going around the room introducing yourselves and saying why you came and what you hope to see come out of the meeting. Some groups use this method at the end also, to keep in touch with the feelings of everyone there. (How did you feel about it? Did you get what you came for?) If the group is large, at least send around an attendance sheet, and alert the more active corps to make a special effort to talk to newcomers at a break or afterward.

(5) *Space consciousness.* Check the seating to make it fit the style and mood you want. Togetherness? Seat everyone close and informal. Let leadership merge with the masses. Success? Space should be a little tight so it feels crowded. Prestige? A well-appointed meeting place with attention to details like flowers.

(6) *Avoid exploitation.* "Joan *likes* to type." Maybe so, but what other choices have been offered her? If no one can stand taking minutes, decide if you really need them. One alternative is to take the last fifteen minutes for a recap of decisions and responsibilities agreed to. This helps pin down assignments, in any case.

(7) *Check up on earlier business.* Responsibility to the collective grows lax when there is no report back. Keeping it lively is a challenge.

(8) *Attend to body language.* An interrupter often can be toned down by turning away toward someone else. Attentive listening to shy ones will encourage participation. Restlessness should signal a change of pace.

(9) *Aphid-eaters.* To find nonpolluting ways of pest control as an alternative to toxic insecticides, some communities are importing "friendly bugs" to eat the aphids. Devise countergames to expose the negative game-playing in your group.

(10) *Different strokes for different folks.* Recognition is the key to a happy membership, but meaningless compliments are boring. Be ingenious in finding ways to recognize everyone's contribution.

(11) *Construct a phoenix out of the ashes.* Suppose you call a meeting of fifteen, and only five come. Don't blame yourself, or those who failed to show, or postpone the meeting. Quickly revise the plan and work from what you *do* have. Turn it into an exciting skull session, or role play, or whatever. Make it so much fun that those who missed will be sorry.

(12) *We can.* You may have to prove it to the skeptics the first time. Having done so, you will be in a position to say, "If we could accomplish that, we can also do this." And you'd better believe it.

Criteria for Determining Where Any Group Is At

(Score on a scale from 1 to 10)

Listening to each other
Reaching decisions
Readiness to take responsibility
Eagerness to meet again
Follow-through on responsibilities taken
Respect for one another
Critical evaluation of progress
Learning from mistakes
Incorporating new people
Enjoying themselves

How do you score?

Under 30: Doesn't look too good
30–50: Needs improvement
50–70: Congratulations!
Over 70: Hard to believe

As women, we are all too familiar with what's wrong with *us*. Now the Movement turns the focus outward. We seek redress for society's ills not primarily in ourselves, but "out there." Unfortunately, we still aren't completely convinced. Having seen the light, we expect miracles. When they don't happen, and when our new expectations for ourselves are shattered, we return to the old familiar self-blame. Well, that's not reality. All action falls somewhere in the middle between the dreams that reveal where we want to go and the dreads that arise in the middle of the night.

Positive organizing accepts the present—including ourselves with all our weaknesses, with both our dreams and our dreads—as the necessary prelude for creating the future.

18.
STRATEGY AND TACTICS

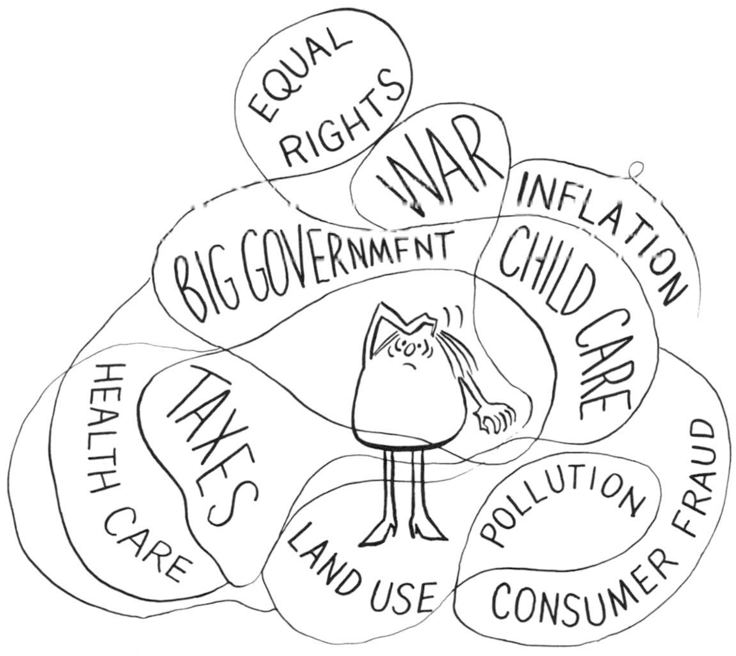

Choosing the Issue

Most of the time we move about with a vague sense of frustration and hopelessness. It's a bad scene. A bad scene is not an issue. The moment that "bad scene" changes to "issue" is when you can do something about it. Since the things we worry about are usually large and complex, finding an issue is not that easy. Who wants to waste a lot of time and effort at risk of alienating friends and family, and then accomplish nothing? Apathy is much less not caring than not believing.

We can all point to prodigious amounts of energy expended with no immediate results—long-range affects perhaps, but most people want to see a tangible payoff. Without success, they become disillusioned with activism. Long-range goals have to be balanced with immediate objectives, but to mobilize people we need to win a few.

First distinguished between a bad scene and an issue:

Bad Scene	Issue
Women with small children who want to work are worried about leaving their children all day with makeshift childcare.	Specific childcare project or Proposal for part-time jobs for women in city government.
Thousands of children die each year from swallowing household drugs.	Zero in on unsafe aspirin packaging.
Treatment of the aged in this country is a disaster area. The end of the extended family, poverty, and technology geared to the young have destroyed the dignity of growing old.	Expose conditions and indignities of present nursing home care in the local area or Involve senior citizens in plans for proposed retirement home.

Bad Scene	Issue
The blind are special victims of fund-raising promoters. There are about 800 separate agencies "serving" the blind. Agencies compete for clients, who are then virtually attached to the agency, the very opposite of the supposed objective of making blind persons "independent."	Expose the "charity biz" by documentation and interviews with clients.
Women are treated by Madison Ave. not only as sex objects, but as products for sale. Feminists feel strongly about this.	National Airline's "I'm Margie—Fly Me" campaign puts it all together so blatantly that even non-feminists are offended. Concentrate on National as an "object lesson" to teach ad agencies to watch their step.
Domestic workers are hard to find, because of low pay, low status, and degrading master-servant relationship.	Develop a "Code of Ethics" for household employment more in line with other fields of employment requiring equal skill and ability.
Pregnant teachers are a no-no in most school districts. Babies come from storks. Family planning is seriously curtailed in teachers' domicile.	Change Board of Education rules to permit teachers to work while pregnant.
War is hell. Yet Vietnam continues to drag on while another holiday season approaches.	"No more shopping days 'til peace." A campaign for a non-commerical Christmas.

A bad scene leaves people limp and helpless. An issue is a ray of hope. It says "Here's something that can be done. It might not work, but there's a chance, and if we win this one, we can go on to bigger things."

What makes a good issue?

Winability. You can't win 'em all, but in the beginning, when the organization is still unsure of its power, there is nothing like winning one fast. Members say to each other incredulously, "We *did* it!" Next project will be far easier to mobilize. For example, a NOW chapter working for an "affirmative action" program for hiring of women selected as its first target a large co-op organization that ostensibly was member-controlled. More susceptible to pressure than most firms, the issue was won—not too easily, not too hard. Just right.

What's our issue, Doris? A childcare center or a spaying clinic?

Grabs people. Rarely, an issue has universal appeal, but it better make sense to those whose support you need. For example, a citizen's group organized in a suburban town to stop a major commercial-construction plan for offices and garage. They appealed to tenants who were distressed because of the housing shortage, to car owners irritated with congestion, to traditionalists and tree lovers, and even to competing business interests. The "superblock" was shut out.

Good guys/bad guys. Clear-cut issues are not easy to sort out in our complex, interrelated society. A noble cause for one group usually steps on someone else's toes, and if those toes are also poorly shod, you don't look so righteous. A classic good guy/bad guy issue that was satisfying to almost all of its supporters was the grape boycott. On the one side was a powerless, poverty-ridden minority conducting a masterful campaign for community support around the basic right to share in some of the fruits of their labor. On the other side were the faceless exploiters. Only such a compelling theme could bring success through a national secondary boycott, a very difficult tactic (especially when you consider that most of the boycotters were not acting in their own immediate self-interests).

Symbolic target. The Goliaths of today are huge, and one is about as bad as the other, so which will we throw our stone at? If possible, we choose one with symbolic value that dramatizes the problem as *we* define it. If the question is better employment opportunities for women in industry, we might choose an employer that makes products which women use. If more women in the corporate management is the target, a sewing-machine manufacturer or a cosmetics giant would be eminently suitable. If childcare facilities is the goal, a baby-food manufacturer should help foot the bill.

Latch onto a case that exemplifies a basic inequality. By working on a particularly flagrant example, we can sometimes unmask a myth, such as "we treat everybody equally." For example, one county in California grants paid leave to male employees when their wives have babies (presumably to help out at home when the wife is in the hospital). But when a woman worker gives birth, she is not eligible for leave, and must use vacation time. The bizarre inequality of maternity leave for men but not for women illuminates the fact that work rules are devised with men in mind. Starting with one ludicrous case, one can lead to a more thorough examination of male-female job inequities.

Self-interest. The more people who are directly benefited by the outcome, the stronger the issue. Humanitarian appeals have more validity in a woman's world than in the "real" one, but if the campaign will require sustained effort, there had better be strong personal motivation to keep it fueled.

Suppose we want the community college to set up a model childcare center for students, staff, and neighborhood. Generating enough pressure to gain support of the administration is only the first step. Then follows the tedious and complicated tasks of funding, which usually requires institutional and government aid. We will have to cope with guidelines, permits, and the myriad problems that we didn't think of when the idea was only a glint in someone's eye. As in bringing babies into the world, the moment of conception is not the hard part—it's the follow-through. For this, we need enough people with a direct personal stake (such as frantic mothers) willing to perform miracles in order to reap the benefits.

Builds organization. Many an issue is but a single step in a complex chess game. Say we are a group of ecology-minded women. We have sponsored a variety of community education activities, such as a speakers' bureau and how-to materials. But it has all been somewhat routine, and we want more impact. There is a particular bill before the state assembly that we consider a must, and we develop a dramatic, newsworthy campaign around that issue for two reasons: to pass that bill, and to build the organizational clout to elect a strong ecology legislator. We may not be influential enough to get the bill passed on our own, but a vigorous campaign will put us on the ecology map. At the same time, we will attract action-minded members; now we can participate in an ecology coalition with some independence. That means our opinions will be listened to, and in mixed company, that's an achievement.

Builds allies. Each group that organizes has a community of interest that overlaps with many other groups'. No one sector can get very far without alliances. Therefore, in defining one's constituency, be very conscious of the needs of others. Women are usually quite good at this, at times bending over backward in trying to see the viewpoint of their protagonists. That's not what I mean. Rather, we need to be far more sensitive to the interests of our potential allies, and tougher with our adversaries.

For example, a group of suburbanites are very interested in new career opportunities for women. Many of them hire weekly household help so that they can take courses or carry on organizational activities. In the same community there is a branch of the National Committee for Household Employment, a combination of lobby group, training program, placement service, and grievance committee for domestic workers. Suppose the middle-class group were to invite a member of that committee to a meeting to see if some common ground for legislative support could be found:

"We'll work for your bill if you'll work for ours." Building on such an alliance might cost the suburban women a few dollars in higher wages. But in the long run, their career chances are brighter. Beyond the dollars is shared humanity.

Necessary Homework

Good issues don't grow on trees; they have to be worked for. It is quite easy to define the bad scene, but it takes considerable digging to uproot an issue. In the process of that digging, the issue is refined.

Take a look across the following chart. The group moves from the bad scene to what appears to be an issue. Then comes the homework. Only after detailed study is that issue sharply enough defined to zero in.

Bad Scene	Suggested Issue
Old age: "Consumer fraud, inflation, fixed pensions, street crimes, absence of mass transit, spiraling rents and housing costs, swelling medical and drug bills and the virtual end of the extended family unit. . . ." (Ralph Nader describes the lot of an old person on a low income in the city.)	Nursing-home care.
While women volunteers go regularly to give service at a local hospital, low-income youth have no access to these hallowed halls except as patients.	With plenty of work to be done, why can't Neighborhood Youth Corps' (NYC) young people be assigned to the hospital?
Commercial TV for children. Hucksterism is rampant with little or no control. Vitamin pills are treated like candy, overpriced and repulsive toys are touted. The programs are bad enough, but the hardcore commercials are even worse.	Why isn't something done about it? Where are the regulatory agencies?
Low-income women over 30 who want to improve their lives are discouraged from entering college-degree programs. Cost, location of school, years required to graduate—all play a part. There is inadequate counseling, no credit for life experience, few opportunities to make up deficient subjects, topped by childcare expenses. If they overcome all these hazards, they get tracked into "women's fields," for which there may or may not be jobs.	Project Second Start: Guidelines for improved adult-education programs for low-income women with children.
Women can deduct only $600 in childcare costs while businessmen and professionals can subtract full cost of their work expenses. There is no adequate childcare available at reasonable prices; therefore, if a woman has to support her children, the burden is on her. On top of that, her pay is on the average half of what a man makes.	Full tax deduction for child-care costs.

Homework	Issue Refined
A group of young women college students applied for jobs at nursing homes. They kept detailed diaries of food, health care, services (or lack of them), and all the small indignities.	Concrete proposals for more stringent codes, more inspectors, withholding of funds from homes that do not comply.
Meetings with NYC, urging selection of youth interested in medical careers; meetings with hospital administration, sympathetic doctors, and those who might be uneasy.	Detailed proposal for summer "mini-internships" for NYC youth, financed by Department of Labor.
Monitor children's programs carefully. Take notes on all offensive characteristics. Time commercials. Analyze what ideas and products are presented to children. Find out what regulatory agencies are supposed to do.	Prepare evidence to force the Federal Trade Commission to do its job. At next public hearings, demand that advertising of drugs and vitamins directed to children be stopped.
Exploratory study of experiences of low-income women with children in adult education evening programs at local college. Three women conduct in-depth interviews to further define educational needs. Examination and evaluation of existent programs at this school, and comparison with innovative programs elsewhere.	Recommendation for improvements of local college's programs. Proposed model (with need documented) for program that takes into account the special problems of working women with children.
Find a case that exemplifies this inequity. *Example:* A widowed secretary, sole support of a two-year-old pays $4,000 in child care from her $9,000 salary at an Eastern law firm. She can deduct only $600. A lawyer at the same firm attends the ABA convention in London at cost of $5,000. He can deduct entire expense of this pleasant trip as a legitimate business expense.	Bill to rectify this tax inequity (e.g., HR9565).

19.
PLANNING THE STRATEGY

Now what do we do? We've moved from the bad scene to a specific issue. We could just start out and play it by ear—take the first step and see what happens. Let the other side react and then come in swinging.

Or, we can try to look ahead a few steps. Anticipate support and opposition, and prepare for a series of moves.

Either way, a strategy is a plan for a campaign. It may unfold in the process of struggle, be prepared in advance, or, better still, evolve as a combination of planning and spontaneity. In any case, it helps to ask the kind of questions that break a strategy down into its parts.

Questions to ask when planning strategy:

What principle is at stake? The clearer you can state it, the more convincingly you can present it—in leaflets, press statements, to other groups, wherever necessary.

What could be accomplished? The goals—short and long range—must be clear enough to muster support. The more tangible and realistic, the better.

Who is with us? Why? Whether a formal alliance is planned or not, your potential supporters will be a factor in the outcome. Who stands where on this issue?

Who is against us? Why? Vital. Start with pocketbook motivation.

Where do we fit in? What is our turf? There may be other organizations already in the field. Sound them out to determine what special role you could play. Rather than duplicate effort, can you appeal to a different constituency?

Where do we start? The first tactic should serve to mobilize the group into action. Since its chief function is to stimulate involvement, the idea should generate enthusiasm.

The Ideological Peg

What makes a campaign score? One essential is a concept that grabs—a theme that strikes a chord of discontent—sometimes expressed in a slogan, a principle of law, or an idea whose time has come. This is the peg that crystallizes all the wrongs into a new "right." "No taxation without representation" launched our republic, and it is reappearing today, expressed by women and minorities. Dozens of these slogans flourish on bumper strips and buttons. If they catch on, they provide a handle for action.

Defining the principles in your terms is taking the offensive in the semantic contest at the heart of social conflict. Is it murder of the unborn for the social convenience of a woman unwilling to take responsibility for her sexual pleasure, or a woman's right to control her body, including unwanted fetuses? For that matter, is it an abortion law or a forced-pregnancy law? Is it growth for a higher standard of living and more jobs, or environmental brinkmanship? Are we environmental doomsayers or protectors of the coming generation? Is it an ever increasing GNP to overcome scarcity and to create abundance, or an age of concrete and congestion? Is it socialized medicine—a revolutionary concept bordering on communism—or is health care a matter of right?

Never let the opposition define the terms for us. We'll be on the defensive from then on. Make the other side run.

Sample Strategy

BAD SCENE: The California state welfare system has become more and more intolerable, particularly for recipients. It is under pressure both by politicians who are exploiting the discontent of taxpayers, and by welfare lawyers and recipient organizations who are pressing for full benefits allowed by law. The patchwork of regulations, and "categories" of the "deserving poor" (blind, disabled, aged, children), do not reflect present-day realities, such as job-

WHAT ARE YOU DOING?
PROTECTIVELY REACTING

lessness. The bulk of recipients are women and their dependent children, victims of a society that assigns them little worth. While liberals discuss federal alternatives, the welfare department is in a state of shock, and poor women have nowhere to turn but to the churches for handouts.

ISSUE: The state welfare system has got to go. An adequate federal assistance program that fills more, not fewer, human needs is overdue.

PRINCIPLE: The poor are organizing to fight for their needs in the same manner as other sections of the population. Welfare is not a charity, but a right. We are all on some form of public assistance. Most women are personally poor; most adult poor are female. But even were this not so, common humanity demands advocacy for those in greatest need.

IDEOLOGICAL PEG: A guaranteed income—or jobs that pay a decent wage.

WHAT COULD BE ACCOMPLISHED? Added pressure for a federal solution to the "welfare mess." Working relationships between poor and middle-class women. Explosion of welfare myths used by politicians who use poor people as scapegoats.

How? By turning tables on the bureaucrats. Accuse the accusers.

Step 1. Work with welfare-rights organizations in the area as well as sympathetic welfare lawyers. Discuss and plan the strategy *together*. Proceed only if in agreement.

Step 2. Hold a public hearing, chaired by a sympathetic congressperson if possible. Call witnesses: recipients with varied problems, social workers, and persons marginally eligible for aid (like working-poor or middle-aged women without dependent children). Present evidence: rats, welfare meal based on current assistance rates, tangle of contradictory regulations (visible examples). Propose legislative change: Have materials available for urging federal legislation (petitions, letter-writing equipment, leaflets, fact sheets, etc.). Special attention to press and media coverage, to insure greatest impact for the effort.

Step 3. Consolidate relationship with recipients by planning next steps together. Future steps might include tangible help in organizing a buying co-op, lobbying plans for the next legislature.

MY KIDS AND I
HAVE TO GO ON WELFARE
ON THE PUBLIC DOLE...
I FEEL SO INADEQUATE

DON'T FEEL INADEQUATE, GRACE~
GOV. REAGAN, LOCKHEED, AND THE
FORD FOUNDATION ARE ON THE PUBLIC DOLE
--- AND THEY DON'T FEEL INADEQUATE

20.
THE CRISIS THEORY OF SOCIAL ACTION

Because I live in earthquake country, I am inclined to think of social change in seismic terms. Tensions build up along the fault line. The earth moves in one direction on the left side, in opposition on the right. The stress increases, unless relieved by small, "friendly" quakes. Without relief, sooner or later there comes a violent upheaval. The earthquake is coming, and some say it is long overdue.

Crises are not all bad—in fact, without them we would hardly get anywhere at all. What's good about a social emergency?

Suddenly we face up to what we knew all along. For example, following the death of Dr. Martin Luther King, Jr., civil rights legislation was passed all over the country after years of foot-dragging. The Kent State tragedy produced a surge of peace action, even inside the Capitol. A crisis clarifies the issue. Water pollution is a bad scene, but when fifty-one thousand fish died from dumping pesticides in an Alabama river, the Geigy Chemical Company stood out as the clear target. Ecologists had been crying out about that river for a long time—now at last they were heard. A hard way to learn, perhaps, but we are willing to cope with catastrophes. Slow erosion is much harder to deal with.

We become more human. During the New York power shut-offs, observers reported the marked change in human behavior toward friendliness and concern for fellow man or woman. When beaches are threatened with sludge, hippies and straights work together in harmony. Disaster seems to bring out the best in us.

We see things in a new perspective. Like an electric shock, our mixed-up value systems get a jolt. There is often a sudden flash of insight, revealing where our true interests lie, and material clutter for an instant has little value compared to our common survival.

The moment of crisis is fleeting, however, a brief period when people want action and need leadership. Emotionally aroused, they look for an effective way to move forward and together. If frustrated, violence may follow, which in turn splits a spontaneous movement. When the crisis is passed, the movement dies—*unless actions are organized.*

When the Crisis Comes, Move Out with the Action

No amount of study can substitute for the emotion engendered by direct experience. Take others with you to the center of things, and participate, talk, feel, work along with everybody else. Because your group has done the homework, try to help others sort out the forest from the trees by asking organizing questions: What happened? Why did it happen? Who is responsible? What can be done—now, tomorrow, and for the future? Find a starting point for congealing the emotion into forward movement. Whoever else is into it, no matter how prestigious, there is something special you can contribute in your own orbit.

A crisis to illustrate was the San Francisco Bay oil spill of January 1971. One foggy night, two Standard Oil tankers collided, dumping 800,000 gallons of crude oil into the bay. Wildlife was seriously endangered, the beaches imperiled, and the citizens enraged. The plight of the sea birds caught public imagination, and there was an outpouring of volunteers to the beaches to rescue the beleaguered coastal bird. Bolinas Lagoon became a special area of concern, with citizens waging what they described as "the Dunkirk of ecology" to save the feeding grounds of the last major colony of great blue herons and white egrets.

All the positive reactions to a crisis were there. People faced up to the real and present danger to their environment. They were very human. Straight persons expressed over and over their admiration for hippie participants, who worked tirelessly with them, and vice versa. For the whole community there was briefly a new insight on the ecology question, a realization that the prophets were indeed speaking truth. Standard Oil became the common enemy.

The second day of the crisis the San Francisco *Chronicle* featured a story about a Bolinas teacher, Erika Zettl, who was pictured with her clothes black with grime from rescuing oil-soaked birds. Erika, who teaches seventh and eighth grades, had been on the beach since 9 A.M. with her students. "We're an ecology-minded school," she said, "and when we heard about it, we wanted to help." With the permission of the school superintendent, the teacher and her students worked all day trying to save the birds, although few were expected to survive.

I don't know Erika Zettl, but I think she acted as any committed person does at time of crisis. She did what she could. I wondered about the follow-up, and imagined how it might have been organized.

A strategy for Erika Zettl

BAD SCENE: Increasing threat to ecological balance of Bolinas Lagoon by man in general and industry in particular.

ISSUE: (1) Save the birds from the oil. (2) Protect the beach and its living things.

WHO IS WITH ME? WHY? My class. Their parents. My whole school. The Superintendent. All those others out on the beach. Conservationists. Boat owners. Ecology-minded unorganized people of all ages.

WHO'S OPPOSED? WHY? Anybody who has to pay costs, specifically the industries affected, and eventually taxpayers.

WHAT IS MY IDEOLOGICAL PEG? "Defenders of the tidal-pool." (That's what we'll call ourselves.)

WHERE DO I FIT IN? WHAT IS MY ORBIT?: My school, parents, and community. Ecology education. My personal involvement and that of others I know. Also, I should tie in with the movement to prevent future spills.

WHERE AM I HEADED? I want to deepen the understanding of those in my orbit of what is really at stake. I stand with those concerned for all of life, against the polluters and spoilers.

WHERE DO I START? First I'll call a Defenders of the Tidal Pool gathering of the children, parents, and anyone else interested, especially those who were out on the beach. At the school perhaps. As soon as possible. We'll talk over things we could do. Some possibilities are preparing a tidal pool exhibit to demonstrate the ecological chain and show how fragile it is. We could make

Bolinas Lagoon a school focus. Here is a chance for the teachers, the children, and the community to work together on something we all feel strongly about. We might plan several meetings, so we can see our tidal pool in its broader context. We'll invite someone from the Sierra Club to discuss their legal battles with us. Some of us might be able to attend a hearing. Also, we should hear about the affects of mercury pollution and pesticides on our tidal pool and what is being done to stop them, if anything. We'll want to know about the legislative picture, but simply explained so our children can understand too. Perhaps there is someone who would help us draft a bill to protect our tidal pool and others like it. It would be good experience for us, and we could take it to our legislator and see what he did about it. If he decides to sponsor it, we can follow it all the way and support it. We might even testify and bring our exhibit.

Erika's instincts were *right on.* First she was ready ("we're an ecology-minded school"). She and her group moved fast ("when we heard about it, we wanted to help"). She took the initiative ("the superintendent gave permission"). She grasped the most crucial issue: the seabirds ("I rescued five birds and one of the boys saved fourteen"). Besides, she had the good fortune to be where the reporter and photographer could make her a symbol of concerned citizens, so that she was in a position to take some leadership.

That is reacting to the crisis. The next task is to carry it on. The strategy suggested is not a blueprint, because organization consists primarily of grabbing opportunities that present themselves—reacting and counterreacting. A strategy is like an outline: something to have in mind to help sort out the questions and the possibilities, but to be responsive to changes in the situation. It should provide enough structure to allow maximum creativity. Try for *planned spontaneity.*

"Where do I start?" That's the crucial question. Once started, the imagination begins to roll.

21.
TACTICS

The late Saul Alinsky—as he would have been the first to admit—was a man. He also happened to be an organizational theorist who was much maligned but often imitated. But he was a man. His style was based upon the most masculine of traits: aggressive confrontation. The question is, are his rules on tactics applicable for women who want to affect social policies? Or, better yet, can they be adapted?

Alinsky's Rules for Tactics Feminized

§ *Never go outside the experience of your people* (those whom you are organizing). What are women familiar with? Shopping. Possible tactics:

(1) large-scale return of credit cards (stores have a mystical attachment to these);

(2) a mass shop-and-return; order c.o.d., then do not accept the merchandise;

(3) tie up personnel on a major shopping day without buying anything; hold a wig-in; tie up dressing rooms. The list stretches as far as the imagination.

WARNING: Even these mild confrontation tactics are difficult for many women, unless they are very angry or deeply concerned with the issue. Such tactics go against the grain of our rearing, and would be more acceptable after other methods had failed. Still, the experience of using whatever power one possesses can be as emancipating for a woman as a karate class.

§ *Wherever possible, go outside the experience of the enemy.* Militant feminists have had great success with this principle. In

New York, when young women whistled at construction workers, made remarks about their physiques, and generally reversed roles, the men retreated to their trucks to eat their lunches. This was a situation completely outside the experience of these men; they were thrown off balance. (If the tactic were repeated too many times, though, its effectiveness would be diminished.) The sympathetic response to the action by women all over the country, who told the story time and time again with great glee, showed that it struck a chord with many who themselves would not have dared to be so bold.

§ *Ridicule is man's most potent weapon.* Woman's, too. When you don't have power or physical strength or conventional weapons, you use your wits. A hallmark of the Women's Liberation Movement is its biting humor, directed against the media image ("Be more of a woman, wear belly-button baubles"), against flagrant sexist journals like *Playboy* ("a woman reading *Playboy* feels a little like a Jew reading a Nazi manual"), and in its catchy picket signs at demonstrations.

Patsy Mink, Representative from Hawaii, made mincemeat of Dr. Samuel Berman, when this highly placed adviser to President Nixon made his famous statement about not wanting a woman in the White House because her judgment would be affected by "raging hormonal imbalances." Comments from women around the country started a flap that cost Dr. Berman his position. The object lesson was not lost on other politicians, who are now more likely to keep such opinions to themselves. The sharp tongues of the bold new women are weapons to be feared.

§ *A good tactic is one that your people enjoy.* In a campaign for employment of minorities in a drug chain, one woman who had worked for the company revealed the pricing code stamped on each item in the store. Each letter had an assigned number, so that GCA might stand for $3.69, which referred to the cost of that item to the firm. Since it was policy to mark up most merchandise, while offering some items at cost or less to attract customers, a reverse boycott was proposed. The code was disseminated, and people were urged to stock up on merchandise at cost or less, but to buy nothing else. That was a popular tactic! One could feel morally good while picking up a bargain.

§ *The threat is usually more terrifying than the thing itself.* The sudden interest of oil companies and other major polluters in maintaining the environment—as reflected in both their commercials and their annual reports—is less the result of sanctions already imposed upon them than the threat to their continued business-as-usual. Lloyd's of London excluded pollution coverage for policies coming due after September 1971. The new move will affect many of the companies on the *Fortune* 500 list (coal, steel, power, paper, tobacco, food, pharmaceuticals, oil, meat-packing, shipping, soft drinks, and plastics). Environmentalists are up in arms, and litigation surely will follow.

Here is a threat that industrialists understand, and they are working desperately to change their image. Lawsuits are one type of threat; another is consumer action. However, to put force behind any threat, it is essential to be able to back it up. If a group has conducted a strong campaign against one firm, it can approach another company and say: You're next. The threat should be sufficient.

§ *Pick the target—freeze it, personalize it, and polarize it.* A historic fighter for the cause of the underdog was Mother Jones of the United Mine Workers (1830–1929). Besides organizing miners and their wives for half a century, she also battled against child labor. Once she took a group of mill children on tour all over the East. "Philadelphia's mansions were built on the broken bones, the quivering hearts, and the drooping heads of these children." Congress protects railroads but not little children, she stated. After her tour, Pennsylvania passed a child labor law.

Eventually that law would have been passed without a Mother Jones, but undoubtedly her tactic saved years and many young lives. Her target was child labor. She froze it—that is, she was not diverted by those who said, "But isn't the *real* problem the mill system?" She personalized it by bringing people face to face with the human costs of exploitation, and she polarized it by pointing to the Philadelphia mansions and their owners. Mother Jones was still being carted off to jail at 72. At 99 she died, still hated by operators and loved by miners and union people.

§ *Do what you can with what you've got.* What do women have, besides numbers? Because we are overtly powerless, we have developed all kinds of tricks to get our way, as any woman knows.

Example one: A proposal for a federal Neighborhood Facilities grant to remodel an old firehouse into a ghetto community center was stalled on the mayor's desk. For some reason, despite many polite requests, it did not move. An amateur actress on the committee for the project offered to wear a floppy hat and "go bug the mayor." For the next week she spent her spare time in the mayor's anteroom and discussed the problem loudly with anyone who entered. It was not long before the mayor signed the proposal and forwarded it to Washington.

Example two: A neighborhood committee presenting a zoning petition to a hostile commission was represented by an Asian woman who presented homebaked fortune cookies to the surprised bureaucrats. With television cameras focused on them, they could not refuse the cookies. "Honorable men are benevolent to worthy petitioners," they read. Forced into a human as opposed to a bureaucratic role, the commission listened to the petition more favorably.

Example three: An overweight woman from Welfare Rights Organization, discussing how to get travel money from an agency for a convention, said, "I'll go sit on his lap. He'll say yes, or go under." Travel funds were provided.

§ *Any attack against the status quo must use the strength of the enemy against itself.* The point here is that Haves fight against not only Have-nots, but also other Haves. Divide and conquer—the oppressor's favorite tactic—can be used against him. Suppose we have two supermarkets across from each other, and each sells a product we are trying to ban. Instead of campaigning against both, even though they may be equally guilty, we pick the more vulnerable and urge customers to do their shopping across the street. This will be infuriating to the manager and confusing to the patrons, but they will be likely to comply because it's so little trouble. It will get results, because the manager can't stand seeing his competitor take his business. That's Alinskyism. It goes against the female grain, but a few victories might change that.

§ *Timing is to tactics . . . the difference between success and failure.* A bus was going to take a group of welfare mothers to the state capital to lobby against a so-called reform bill. Very few women turned out, even though the issue was crucial. An organizer had not taken into consideration that Monday was check day for the mothers. "Their kids are hungry by the end of the month and they're going to get their stamps no matter what else is going on," she realized. Knowing the lifestyle of the people involved is essential to make a tactic work.

Time works both ways. If results are too slow in coming people grow discouraged or bored. On the other hand, when you don't have the power to make policy, you might have enough to cause delay. Suppose a big shopping center is proposed for a piece of waterfront property that you feel should be used for a public park. You may not be able to swing enough support to make city government buy that property, but you can have enough people at a hearing to prevent the required zoning change.

§ *Possessing a rationale gives a meaning and a purpose.* A woman's right to control her own body has given an entirely new meaning to the rapidly changing climate in regard to abortion. Women are petitioning to repeal abortion laws in all states, a prospect that seemed impossible a few years ago. In this case two rationales converged: the growing realization that if population growth is not slowed down we face extinction, and the contention that a woman's body is her own. Despite strong and vocal opposition, the abortion-law-repeal movement is moving along.

§ *Tactics like life require that you move with the action.* The Action Committee for Decent Childcare (ACDC) of Chicago started in January 1971. Frustrated with licensing problems, some 70 women staged at a City Council budget hearing a "baby in" to demand that Chicago commit $12 million for childcare, and a more realistic * demand that the city set up an office of childcare services. From this first action grew an organizing drive and a network of chapters including parents and single women, as well as childcare councils of persons working in centers. Each group is represented on a policy-making steering committee.

With press on hand, ACDC descended on a surprised childcare official on July 26 of that year, forcing the city to accede to a public meeting to air grievances on childcare licensing. ACDC followed up on this victory by organizing massive participation for the public hearing.

Here you find a synthesis of tactics that moved with the situation. A large number of babies at a budget hearing guaranteed a stop to bureaucratic business. At the same time, it allowed the

* "Realistic" here means what you actually can get.

young mothers to be part of the action without having to find baby-sitters. If the children were fussy or cried, so much the better. No need to be embarrassed or carry them out this time! The tactic was fun, and exhilaration from a taste of power carried over to the organizing drive. ACDC picked a target (licensing problems) and froze it within an overall vision (universal, free, parent-controlled, 24-hour childcare). It converted that vision into concrete and winnable objectives or reforms that will do three things:

"(1) Make things somewhat better in reality for women.

(2) Build a base of organization that will give women a sense of their own power.

(3) Somewhat alter the control of irresponsible institutions over women." *

What are tactics? They are tools. Suppose we have an extensive remodeling job to do, and all we have to work with is a screwdriver. We would be very limited in what we could do. The more kinds of utensils we have, the more effectively we can work. That presumes we know how and when to use an assortment, including power tools, and will pick the right one for the job to be done. But so long as women limit themselves to one or two hand tools, we will accomplish little.

Confrontation tactics are only one series of tools. Legal battles have to be waged as well, and exposés, and conferences, and even letter-writing. Persuasion, education, and expressions of public opinion are all necessary, as well as the familiar picketing—to say nothing of throwing the scoundrels out and electing our own women. In organizing, sometimes you settle for the tactic that the group will accept, even though a more daring one would blast a bigger hole in the status quo.

Tactics for the New Woman

Can we learn to work *with* altruism and our other "feminine" characteristics? Is there a womanly style? From a positive viewpoint, our altruistic brainwashing can be a strength in developing

* From ACDC statement.

sisterhood, which isn't an easy task. We can feel compassion for other women in trouble, which is one reason that so many women's centers are developing in larger cities, to help women find housing or perhaps a job—at the least, a sympathetic ear and a chance to rap. This is easier for us than becoming advocates of those in need, which implies conflict and confrontation.

We women are strong on flexibility, and are used to making do. And we're good at psyching out the opposition. Best of all, men are basically afraid of assertive women—something to keep in mind when choosing tactics. It's easier for us to follow the rules than break them, so we should be good at pushing regulations to their limits.

A new aggressiveness is emerging, however. Groups of women are beginning to protect each other. I have witnessed women running to the defense of a sister who has been pushed around, and have seen feminist groups forcibly evict men who would not leave when asked to do so. Physical superiority of males can be compensated for by numbers.

Actually, we have so much going for us that we could spend the next ten years devising creative new tactics. As a matter of fact, we will.

22.
CO-OPT THE SYSTEM

What does it mean to work through the system? To go to the polls and say yea or nay to a proposition? To pick between identical candidates (will the *real* apologist for industrial pollution please step forward)? To work for election of a lesser evil you had no part in choosing? These are old methods that have been tried and found wanting in this generation as in all others.

Or does working in the system mean to press forward to push your best leadership into positions where they might have some influence, then see them co-opted? Whether they are bought out by the promise of a bright personal future, brainwashed by establishment rationale, or disillusioned by continually compromising doesn't much matter. Whatever the cause is, the conditions that led to the reform movement in the first place remain virtually unchanged. The only difference: your leaders are gone.

Some change is brought about by reversing positions, that is, by co-opting the system. The principle is not new, only now it is called by different names—"participatory democracy," for one. The premise is: The system is not monolithic. The establishment *can* be moved; the system *can* be used. In the process of shoving forward, all available hands are needed working in unison, which itself lays the basis for some fundamental restructuring of power relationships. For success, there can be no illusions. Expectations must be tempered with a degree of cynicism. And you can never stop pushing.

Clearly, trying to co-opt the system has grave dangers. A strong argument can be made for staying outside the corrupt and corrupting atmosphere of power. But at this particular moment in history, there are good reasons why women can gain a great deal by tackling institutions head-on and trying to make them work in their own interests:

(1) You have to study the system to find what processes are susceptible to co-optation.

(2) In doing so, women gain confidence in themselves.

(3) Demystification takes place. Women no longer are willing to leave important decisions affecting their lives to "experts."

(4) Some immediate benefits will be achieved, encouraging others to move.

(5) Women will gain admittance into male domains as the establishment tries to co-opt *them* (in some cases successfully), but in so doing, will set precedents for female representation.

Law 'n' Order

Ever since passage of the Civil Rights Act of 1964, women have been doing battle in the courts. Sexism, we have discovered, is institutionalized. Since the laws that affect our institutions are interpreted (and reinterpreted) in court, any solid change includes legal action.

A formula might read: bad scene ⟶ pressure ⟶ legal recourse ⟶ non-compliance ⟶ legal struggle. The same interrelationship between the courts and social action is found in the ecology field, civil rights, poverty, prostitution, and about every other area of human concern. The law is everybody's battleground.

Sue 'Em!

The many activist women going into law will not lack clients. Here are some significant cases in which the legal system is co-opted in the interests of women:

§ The pro-abortion movement has moved from *reform legislation* to *repeal* of restrictive statutes by the courts. In January 1970, 300 women plaintiffs with 6 women attorneys pressed a class-

action lawsuit in Federal Court, challenging the constitutionality of New York State's abortion laws (*Abramowicz vs. Lefkowitz*). The suit was declared moot when the state legislature amended the abortion laws, leaving the constitutional questions unanswered. Is a forced pregnancy involuntary servitude, as prohibited under the Thirteenth Amendment? Do abortion laws, even liberal ones, deny a woman's right to privacy and her right to decide whether or not to bear children as guaranteed in the First, Fourth, Fifth, Eighth, and Ninth Amendments? The suit, and those like it in other states, is for the *right* to obtain an abortion, if and when desired.

§ Shirley Marshall, a stenographer, filed a class-action suit against her employer, Lockheed of Atlanta, Georgia, charging discrimination in hiring, pay placement, promotion, and recruitment. "Plaintiff and the class she represents have suffered immense economic injury. . . . their earnings have been and are far lower than the earnings of males doing comparable work, and their opportunities to be employed have been drastically curtailed by Defendant's sex discriminatory limitation of such work opportunities," the case begins. This suit is based not only on the 1964 Civil Rights Act, but also on an old Reconstruction statute of 1866. If successful, Lockheed women workers will receive back pay making up wage differentials from the time of their initial employment. Unequal pay could be unprofitable!

§ Ecologists and environmentalists are also exploring new legal avenues of struggle. Futurists are beginning to study the legal system with the intensity of a lifer in prison, looking for a way to make the law serve the survival of the earth's resources (and of the earth's inhabitants!). For example, the "Dusty Dissenters" of Fernley, Nevada, recently won a stunning victory. Eighty-five of them were awarded $18,000 apiece in pollution damage from a large cement plant that failed to use a dust precipitator. "A deliberate, wanton disregard for the property of others," said the judge. "The whole country is talking about what we've done," said Helen Smith, one of the Dissenters. (The case will be appealed by the company, as usual.)

§ A ruling that may lead to similar civil action in other states was handed down by a federal three-judge panel in Philadelphia on October 8, 1971. The judges ruled that retarded persons between ages 6 and 21 are entitled "to a free, public program of education and training" appropriate to their learning capacity. Rather than relying on sympathy and volunteers, activists had used the courts to fight for the rights of the retarded. Patricia Clapp, president of the Pennsylvania Association for Retarded Children, which initiated the suit, hailed the ruling as a landmark.

§ The San Francisco Neighborhood Legal Assistance Foundation filed a suit on behalf of women prisoners in county jails. They charged sex discrimination because women are not allowed to participate in work-furlough programs. So long as they cannot do so, they should not be incarcerated in county jails, they argued. "They don't understand our setup. We don't have separate toilet facilities," the officials complained. The petitioners and their legal counsel were of course not concerned with the city's plumbing problems. They were seeking relief for women prisoners, whatever way they could. A formula is presented:

PETITIONERS: We demand our [equal] rights.
OFFICIALS: You don't understand—we're not set up for equality.
PETITIONERS: Then change your setup, because the law says we have equal rights.

The case was won. One floor was set aside for women's facilities.

The same pattern emerges in legal battles over childcare, pregnancy leave, and many types of job opportunities for women. Lack of toilet facilities is a favorite ploy to deter breakthroughs for women (even in the space program). "No room for a childcare center" and "women can't travel" are others.

§ A variation on this theme is conducted by the National Welfare Rights Organization and their legal counsel around the principle of due process. This is a defensive action, using the state's own rulebook to prevent cuts in welfare grants. The law in California provides that the recipient may request a hearing before a cut is put into effect, the assumption being that few persons on welfare will avail themselves of this legal procedure. With the new consciousness of law that prevails, quite the opposite has taken place.

The system is co-opted in that the welfare department is forced to obey its own rules, through the system's own courts. A particularly ironic example of this strategy occurred when a U.S. District Judge stopped California's welfare department from reducing grants because the recipients had not been properly notified of the changes and given a chance of appeal (September 28, 1971). The formula might be written:

RECIPIENTS: We demand our due process, according to your own laws.
WELFARE DEPARTMENT: This represents a great deal of work for us. We have to review the cases all over again, issue retroactive checks, and then take the same action of termination or reduction. [S.F. Dept. of Social Services general manager Ronald Born]

RECIPIENTS: These are *your* rules—we demand you follow them.

Meanwhile, the mother with three children receives her "full" $280 monthly allotment. Also, the welfare rights attorney files cases claiming that the state is causing a jam-up by sitting on fair hearing cases, and is itself guilty of "conspiracy."

§ Sally Reed of Boise, Idaho, thought that a law that regards men as better qualified than women to administer an estate violates the equal-protection clause of the Fourteenth Amendment. "I just cared about the principle of the thing," she said. She carried her fight to the Supreme Court, which in November of 1971 finally recognized equality of women under that amendment. Suffragists had sought in vain such equal protection for the right to vote. "I hope more women will do what I did," Ms. Reed said. "Instead of complaining about the way things are, we've got to go into the courts and get them changed." That legal shift reflects the vigor of the whole women's-rights movement.

The law is what you make of it. If you believe that it can solve all injustice, you are a blind woman who doesn't know that the scales are loaded. "Lawyers are reduced to getting asses out of the injustice wringer one at a time, but they can't stop the wringer," says feminist lawyer Florynce Kennedy.

Approached without illusions, it is a battleground of immense importance. The courts are a part of the power structure in which we have at least a toe-hold. Co-opting the system means make it work for you rather than on you (or over your dead body). It

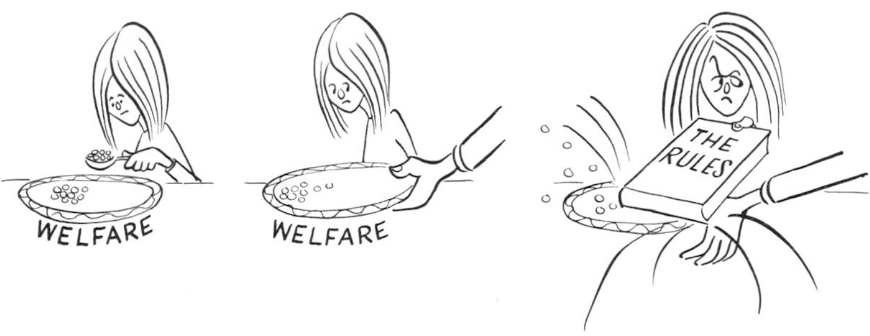

means choosing a particular part of that system, studying the rules, and learning to play the game—without getting caught up in it and getting lost.

Filing charges

As women become more sophisticated about legal usage, they develop tactics to force reluctant holdouts to comply with the law of the land. Threat of suits is one such tactic. The Atlanta chapter of NOW describes its own successful experience with filing charges with the Equal Employment Opportunity Commission (EEOC) with the hope that other women will do likewise.

How We Got the Atlanta Newspapers to De-sexigrate the Want Ads

(1) We met with the newspapers' classified-ad director. Nothing.

(2) We devoted one NOW meeting to filing charges. We took copies of a Sunday paper want-ad section to the meeting and spent the evening cutting out copies of ads, column headings showing "Male Help Wanted" and "Female Help Wanted" listings, and sections showing the name and date of the paper.

(3) We attached copies of the ads with the headings and datelines on EEOC Charge forms. Each member took one of these forms and signed a charge of discrimination against the company or personnel agency whose ads were attached. (We filed charges against many personnel agencies.) The charges went something like this: "XYZ Company [or XYZ Agency] placed this ad under 'Male Help Wanted' in the ——— issue of [name of paper]. I believe that this ad discriminates against me and all females because of our sex."

(4) We sent all these charges at once to the EEOC Office in Atlanta—about 20 charges in all, including some that named several personnel agencies—with the whole page of the paper attached.

(5) When EEOC began to investigate the charges, the personnel agencies consulted with each other and contacted the papers to let them know they'd prefer not to have law suits against them. They had economic clout with the papers, and convinced them to discontinue separate help want-ad columns—

sort of "If we can't advertise by sex, nobody is going to." (While there is still some question about the papers, there is no question about the jurisdiction of EEOC over employers and personnel agencies, and placing a sex-segregated ad is prima facie evidence of sex discrimination.)

(6) Next thing we knew, the "Male" and "Female" heading disappeared with no announcement of any kind. We hope through the ads now to get at the agencies and have their other placement practices investigated . . . we have not signed any agreements or withdrawn the charges; but at least the ads are now all under a single listing.

Important! We did not *apply for the jobs; we did* not *claim to be qualified for them. We simply said the ads discriminated against females. You can do it too:* It's an easy thing to try. It may not work, but we think the threat of suits against companies and agencies which place the ads will make them use their persuasive powers with the papers. If your nearest EEOC office won't take charges on this basis, saying you have to apply for the job, etc., tell them one office did and tell them the outcome. If they still won't, contact the Atlanta NOW Chapter. We'll contact the office here and ask them to get something done about it.

What you need at your meeting: Members to sign charges, a stack of EEOC Charge forms, a supply of newspaper want-ad sections, pens, scissors, stapler, tape and/or glue, some blank sheets of paper to attach ads to. It wouldn't hurt to have a notary public on hand to notarize charges on the spot.

Threading the maze

The System seems so impregnable because it is incredibly complicated, and bureaucrats like it that way. Only the knowledgeable few have the inside track. Boiling down the laws (and the agencies responsible for them) that apply to an issue is essential, preferably *before* being directed from one office to another. This chart, for federal laws covering sex discrimination in employment, shows how.

FEDERAL LAWS COVERING SEX

Law	Coverage	Requirements
Presidential Executive Order 11375 (amending Executive Order 11246)	1. federal government contractors, contracts of $10,000 and up (including educational institutions) 2. federally assisted construction 3. federal employees	1. nondiscrimination in all aspects of employment 2. for contracts of $50,000 and up: plan of affirmative action to remedy affects of past discrimination 3. guidelines of Revised Order #4 require specific goals and timetables for such plans
Civil Rights Act of 1964 Title VII	1. employers of 15 or more persons 2. unions 3. employment agencies (including state) 4. state and local governments	1. nondiscrimination in all aspects of employment: hiring, upgrading, dismissal, terms of employment, referral for employment, membership, apprenticeship, training 2. prohibits companies from advertising in sex-segregated ads 3. nullifies state "protective" laws
U.S. Fair Labor Standard Act	1. industries engaged in interstate commerce 2. all employers subject to minimum-wage standards	1. equal wages for equal work 2. may not reduce wage of one sex to equalize it with that of the other sex
Presidential Executive Order 11478	federal civil-service employment	1. nondiscrimination in all aspects of employment 2. each agency must establish affirmative-action program for equal opportunity

DISCRIMINATION IN EMPLOYMENT *

Exemptions	Enforcement Powers	Jurisdictional Agency(ies)
1. nonfederal contractors 2. nonfederally assisted construction	can fail to award contract or can cancel contract. Department of Justice can enjoin.	Office of Federal Contract Compliance (OFCC) For educational institutions: Health, Education and Welfare For federal employees: Call U.S. Civil Service Commission
religious/ educational institutions	cannot issue cease-and-desist orders. No direct enforcement powers. EEOC attorneys can seek court enforcement.	Equal Employment Opportunity Commission (EEOC)
1. local, state, and federal, government (except hospitals) 2. executive (those earning more than $400/mo.), professional, and administrative employees (including teachers)	back wages may be collected by employee suit or by Secretary of Labor. Repeated violations: criminal charges and $10,000 fine.	Department of Labor: Wage and Hour Division
1. General Accounting Office 2. aliens employed outside limits of U.S.	1. right to a hearing by appeals examiner 2. Board of Appeals and Review, U.S. Civil Service Commission, shall issue final decision.	U.S. Civil Service Commission (or see Director of Equal Opportunity for each agency)

* As of March 1972.

The advocates

Not everyone can or will pore over the laws on the books to glean this kind of information. Even with a chart, it takes help and support to follow through on a grievance. But some women are becoming specialists. They sort out the agencies, help the person or group file a complaint, and provide the kind of encouragement that can spell the difference between giving up and fighting on to success.

The *Women's Advocate Corps of NOW* (Chicago): Sisterly concern, mutual support, paralegal counsel all are provided by this group of feminists to any woman who feels she has experienced discrimination in employment. Each person who seeks help receives personal attention. From her complaint, the issue is defined and the charge filed through the proper agency. If needed, she is accompanied through each confusing step.

The *Women's Job Rights* (San Francisco Bay Area): After-work job clinics are the vehicle this group uses. A collective of women from various professional backgrounds (law, banking, fair-employment consulting, and social work), deeply committed to equal opportunity, pooled their expertise to make the laws against discrimination viable. Minimally funded by Women in Leadership (WIL; United Presbyterian Women), they work out of an office donated for after-business hours. As they describe the project: "The politically uninitiated or timid are assured because it is totally within our current legal framework, and the politically disillusioned can be involved because of the highly personal contact and visible success possibilities—a raise, a promotion, a job."

Co-opter's Glossary

affirmative action A key civil-rights ideological peg. In employment, it means that if a firm is not reasonably representative of the surrounding community, it must act affirmatively to remedy the effects of past discrimination. When applied to women's employment (as a result of Title VII, Civil Rights Act of 1964), affirmative action challenges division of work by sex. When women are in all the low-paid, low-status jobs, it is presumed, by "pattern and practice," that they have been blocked from upgrading, and steps should be taken to overcome past patterns of exclusion. (Isn't that discrimination in reverse? No. One line at the grocery counter is slowed down while the other line catches up.)

class-action suit A legal procedure that has been expanding in recent years, it allows one person or a group to sue as representatives of a whole class of affected persons. Leverage is greatly increased, especially when complainants seek back pay or damages. In ecology cases, for example, damages to thousands of people of $100 each could be a deterrent, where for one person it would be meaningless. Also used effectively by minorities, poverty groups, and women.

contract compliance Once a law is passed, the work shifts to enforcement. For example, most contracts with the federal government require evidence of nondiscrimination (affirmative-action plans with goals and timetables). Although the Office of Federal Contract Compliance has the power to cancel contracts, they use it selectively. All the more reason for pressure by minorities and women.

mandamus action (or writ of mandamus) Means "make 'em do it." An individual or organization goes to court to force the responsible agency to obey the law.

population parity A new ideological peg used by women and minorities. Means there should be more equal representation in the areas that count: jobs, policy positions, and in the democratic process. Goal of affirmative-action programs is to bring each underrepresented segment of the society into parity with their numbers in the population (or work force, in the case of women). Understandably, the concept scares white men.

Revised Order No. 4 Requires federal contractors to set goals and timetables to rectify job discrimination against women, effective Spring 1972. (Don't hold your breath—keep pushing.) Administered through U.S. Department of Labor, Office of

Federal Contract Compliance. Additionally, guidelines forbid employers from advertising in "male" or "female" help-wanted columns. Also, employers must make reasonable provisions for maternity leave. A woman must be allowed to return to work after childbirth without loss of service credits. Also, employers may not deny employment to women with young children unless the same applies to men.

23. MASS MEDIA: THE BELOVED MONSTER

News ⟶ attention ⟶ changes the climate ⟶ makes change possible. A useful formula that all activists keep in mind. But here's another one:

Power ⟶ distorts media ⟶ controls the climate ⟶ prevents change. Equally true. So move down the center, keeping both in mind. No illusions, but no fear either. Learn to co-opt the media, using whatever cracks and crannies you can get your fingernails into. Use—but don't be used.

Here's where creativity comes in, and the fun of struggle. Avoid the obvious. When an action is discussed, think "news value" and devise a tactic that will (1) get you the best coverage, and (2) educate at the same time.

What's News?

Something new, or significant, or of special local interest. Names are news, especially well-known ones. Numbers are good, and anything unusual that catches attention. The "first" of anything is news. A news story describes events, and on the surface at least is objective. News is now, not last week.

Orchestrate the News

Except for routine publicity for events, women's groups seldom see themselves as newsmakers, but activists should think of themselves as that. "News consciousness" sees the action as inseparable from media, plays all the angles, judges possible responses, and organizes news personnel as part of the team. *Questions:* What do we want to get across? How can we dramatize it or make it newsworthy? Who do we know in the media on our side? How do we set it up? Don't be a little triangle ready to clink at the nod of an establishment conductor. Orchestrate your own tune.

"Sex Sells"

A group of women artists, irritated that the director of the University of California Art Museum had ignored their request for more representation for their sex, caught the museum in a goof. A photographic exhibit of Storyville prostitutes was scheduled for the museum on March 8, 1972—International Women's Day. (On the Berkeley scene this event had been honored for the previous two years with large women's conferences.) Among the photos were some used by pimps in the legalized New Orleans red-light district of 1912—artistic, but depicting women in the traditional supine role. The art group contacted all the media, notifying them of an action on the opening day. At the appointed time more media representatives than pickets showed up, but the event received national coverage—a nice, juicy story. Twenty minutes after picketing began, the museum agreed to the artists' demands. This group turned sex-sell to its own advantage.

Seize the Time

When opportunity knocks, don't call out, "I'll be with you later." Use that precious moment in the spotlight to best advantage. Think of Deborah Jean Sweet, who, when handed a Young Americans Medal by Richard Nixon for her part in a march to buy food for poverty-stricken children, said on national television, "I can't believe in your sincerity in giving these awards for service until you get us out of the Vietnam war." This brave high-school student later told reporters she refused to be used as a symbol of satisfied young Americans.

Table-Turning Techniques That Make News

Since reversals of the ordinary are what brings the media running, we should know how to create them. "Man bites dog" is how news is defined, isn't it?

Reversal, like satire, points to a new perspective on truth. The shoe is on the other foot, so we are forced to test the fit. Very often reversals turn power relationships upside down, and in so doing give the underdog new courage. They sometimes spotlight how grotesque our priorities are. Turning the tables is one way to make a point and news at the same time. Here are two table-turners:

§ The *Citizens Organization for a Sane World* staged a "spy-in" at Secretary of Defense Melvin Laird's Bethesda, Maryland, home to protest alleged surveillance by CIA and Army agents of antiwar homes. They used a "spyscope," Sherlock Holmes pipes, and other such trappings to create a newsworthy picture, which then went out on the AP wire service. There were probably not more than six persons involved, but they made their point with enough imagination to warrant a nationwide wire photo.

§ The *California Welfare Rights Organization* presented Governor Ronald Reagan with an award for being "the biggest welfare recipient of us all." The presentation was made before TV cameras in a situation that the governor could not dodge. Following close on the disclosure that he had paid no state income tax that year due to "business reversals," the award had fine news value. It was thoroughly enjoyed by the beleaguered recipients, and served notice to other politicians that the powerless were learning new tricks.

When in doubt about how to proceed, try turning the whole cake upside down. You may find pineapple on the top.

Madison Avenue on Our Side?

No, but every branch of the establishment has its friendlies. If the medium is the message, it might as well be our message.

§ "Help Unsell the War" provides a series of ads for every type of media (TV spots, layouts geared to magazines and newspapers, radio tapes, posters). Prepared by peace-oriented admen and women, it is distributed through Clergy and Laymen Concerned. Their purpose is to counter the twelve thousand radio and television tapes and two million printed releases distributed by the Army's Hometown News Center in Kansas City, as reported in "The Selling of the Pentagon." The campaign urges people to act. "Let's not just wind it down, for God's sake, let's wind it up."

§ Women professionals in the advertising field are preparing a feminist campaign for NOW. When completed, it will include television commercials, radio tapes, magazine engravings, and newspaper mats. The advertising campaign promotes employment and educational opportunities for women and compliance with laws against sex discrimination, and discourages sex-role stereotyping. It's central theme is womanpride.

§ Ad Lib is an underground movement on Madison Avenue designed to end the slurs and putdowns to women in today's advertising. It may not be too obvious as yet, but the women on the inside are pointing to their protesting sisters outside and telling their bosses, "Get with it. Women are changing, and sexism doesn't pay anymore."

When Madison Avenue invites you in to look at its echings, by all means accept, but keep the door open for a hasty retreat or you may be seduced.

Meet the Press

Public-relations or press person is a vital job in any organization, and there are too few willing and able to perform it. The job involves work and responsibility, but also rewards. Pitch in and learn. This is the person who will write news releases, notify the media of events that should be covered, and handle press conferences. To do the job well, she will get to know some reporters and learn as much as she can about the local media. She will develop a nose for news to better help the group be media wise.

Deadlines are what we all have, but newspapers most of all. For cooperation from press, learn to respect their work problems.

Hitchhike on the news. When you see a story that relates to your field, come right in there with a statement. If someone makes a negative comment, use the fairness doctrine to get your side across. Call in immediately, "Our organization strongly disagrees with the statement by ———. We feel that . . ." Stay cool.

Photos help any story. A speaker coming? Ask for a picture (glossy). If possible, deliver to the newspaper in person. (And have a stamped return envelope if you want it back.)

Wire services are used by all the media. If your story is used by one, it will be sent out nationally and to radio and TV stations.

Reporters are people. Treated like other human beings with respect but not awe, they can be very helpful. Women reporters are really worth cultivating.

Women's pages are disappearing (just as we were beginning to get some stories in them!). Integration is a good thing only if our news is carried elsewhere in the paper and women reporters don't get shafted. The "women's news" ghetto is usually still there underneath the up-to-date "family living" title. Help change its content by bombarding them with *your* stories.

Press conferences are called to notify all the press of something significant. Which means there should be a figure of national stature involved, an important statement of policy, or a new project to be launched. If you blow it by calling a press conference for something trivial, you will lose credibility with your media friends. Send out invitations several days in advance, if possible, and remind by phone. Have a press packet on hand: a copy of the speech or statement, a fact sheet, group background literature, and data on the speaker. Be prepared for probing questions. Don't be defensive or hostile—it's a reporter's job to probe. A multimedia press conference will have the greatest impact.

The news release—bread and butter of press work

If the story is newsworthy, and you write it up following their rules, it will fare better:

• Be completely "objective." If any opinions are expressed, put them in quotes, attributing them to yourself if necessary.

• Answer the questions: who, what, where, when, why, and how in the first paragraphs. Stories are generally cut from the end.

• An individually typed story, with SPECIAL TO [NAME OF PAPER] on the top will improve your chances. Don't send the same story to another paper.

• If time is short, deliver in person.

Sample Press Release

Organization Letterhead

For further information contact:

Lois Winter	*name*
Press Secretary	*title*
234 55th St.	*address*
Oakland, Ca. 94601	
543-2222 (office)	*phone(s)*
567-3454 (home)	

FOR IMMEDIATE RELEASE

space

The Women's Action Center will hold a	*who, what*
public meeting at Lucy Stone Hall in Truth	*where*
Park, on Tuesday, February 15, at 8 P.M. to	*when*
celebrate Susan B. Anthony Day. The program	*why*
will feature a dramatic presentation depicting	*how*
highlights from the suffragist's life.	

# # #

[or –30–] *signifies end*

Radio Is Not Dead

Because television is where the big money goes, radio is a lot easier to penetrate. Local stations are often eager to have lively content: talk shows, interviews, debates, spots, poetry. If you will do the work to prepare interesting material, many stations are likely to be cooperative. Talk to the program manager. College stations are a good bet, if there's one in your area.

But some women have gone further than that. KPFA in Berkeley is a listener-sponsored station of the Pacifica Foundation (as is WBAI in New York). Very much with it, the station seeks to provide valid and lively radio for its wide and loyal audience. In 1971 a woman's collective, composed of staff (mostly clerical) and volunteers, decided to change the standard sex roles. They wanted to learn the technical side of the trade, and they were quite willing to show the men how to manage some of the clerical duties. They pushed for special women's programming, which became a popular daily series, *Unlearning To Not Speak*. This now includes a whole spectrum of styles and subjects, a weekly women's newscast, poetry, and music. In the process, women are learning broadcasting from A to Z.

We Can Talk Back to Our Televisions

They may not listen very well but at least we can nag. Former FCC Commissioner Nicholas Johnson, among others, tells us how. Essentially, it boils down to habitually writing stations, advertisers, commentators, and the rest of them; studying how the medium works and hoisting them by their own petard. Push hard on the fairness doctrine in the handling of controversial issues of public importance, as interpreted by the Federal Communications Commission. While the FCC is not an effective guardian of our interests, they can be moved, as can advertisers and station managers.

All over the country blacks, Chicanos, consumerists, environmentalists, war dissenters, Women's Liberationists, Gay Liberationists, and others are demanding air time, more say about news coverage, and equality in hiring practices. Furthermore, they are challenging station licenses. John A. Schneider, president of the CBS Broadcast Group, said he fears that some of the special-interest organizations want not only access, but to change the medium. "It's like acupuncture," he said in a Washington *Post* interview. "People are sticking those needles in me for my own good. Everyone wants to perform corrective surgery."

So now is a good time to be assertive. Whatever your issue, put in your needle. "Public service" means us.

§ The Committee for Open Media in the San Francisco Bay area started from Arnold Toynbee's comment "You have to shoot somebody, burn yourself alive, do something violent, in order to get any attention at all, however good your cause, however patient you have been, however well you have put your case." For several months the Committee negotiated with local television stations for public access in prime time for controversial ideas. At the time of this writing, three stations had acceded to 50-second spots, taped and aired at the stations' expense, to promote communication from people to people. Not much time, but an important beginning, and the Committee was soliciting organizations to use it.

§ One group that followed through was the South Bay (California) chapter of NOW. Their 50-second commercial, presented on local TV at no expense, shows how to get a message across in a brief spot:

> A woman is seated with a boy at her side and a girl on her lap. She says, "Hello, my name is Enid, and these are my two children. But only one will learn that the world is wide open. Only one child might become an astronaut or the president, and only one will earn enough money for self-support. The other child will have a very different future. The other will be told about the proper way to live. Only the lowest-paying jobs will be offered, and the chances are much greater that the other child will be on the welfare rolls. One child is my son—the other, my daughter. The National Organization for Women is fighting for the other child. [Name, address, and phone number of local chapter flashes on screen.] Join us."

Media of Our Very Own

With the launching of Gloria Steinem's magazine *Ms.,* a new television show on WCBS called *Woman!,* and radio programs on the pattern of the KPFA show, the question arises, how will female media differ from the establishment/male way of doing things? Will they? One point all three of the above have in common is a serious desire to overcome male pyramidism. Status work and drudgery is shared; everyone answers phones, makes coffee, types letters. Nicholas Von Hoffman, Washington *Post* columnist, says, "If this kind of organization catches on, it could destroy the American businessmen, those pointy-headed pharaohs atop Steinem's pyramid who count coups and score prestige points by the number of secretaries and receptionists who wait on them." There you would have an alternative structure right in the middle of the establishment.

The media may be a monster, but with more of us inside, it can be tamed. To break in, follow the three-point formula: learn—dare—do.

24.
THE QUEEN'S ENGLISH, OR LINGUISTIC ACTIVISM

Thought is molded by language. In turn, language is altered by new thought. Every movement adds new terms to our vocabulary and attacks others. Blacks redefined the word "nigger" from an epithet to the black experience in white America. A whole spate of new words—ecotactics, terracide, biosphere—has been created by ecologists. Chicanos fight for their native tongue as an instrument of identity, starting with the word "Chicano." But no movement will have as great an impact on English as the Women's Movement, for the very fabric of our language reinforces male supremacy, as feminists are discovering. As consciousness rises, more and more of us become linguistic activists.

Subsuming: out from under. Women are supposedly included in general terms like "man," "mankind," or "person," but certainly not on an equal basis, in either law or life. Pronouns (the generalized "he," for example) are the worst culprits. Feminists are working to get out from under that ubiquitous "he," but language is slow to change, and it's hard to come to agreement on substitutes. The ear must be retrained.

Feminist lexicographer Varda One suggests "ve," "vis," "ver" for pronouns referring to both sexes. Mary Orovan goes back to Indo-European roots and comes up with "co" (which already means "together"), which she declines: "co," "co's," "co," and "coself," referring to either sex. Sound strange? Of course, but, as she points out, pronouns are among the first words a child learns. The next generation of children should learn early that they live not in a "he-man" universe, but in a human one. "They," "their," "theirs," and "themself" have also been suggested for all situations that need a neutral pronoun in singular as well as plural.

In this book I've tried to avoid the sexist pitfalls by using "she," since I'm writing about women. But when that doesn't work, I've found "they" the easiest substitute. Prediction: The Women's Movement will eventually eliminate the subsuming pronouns, but not without sweat and tears, and trial and error.

"Manglish" reforms. Besides pronouns, our language assumes that leadership roles are male. But this is now challenged. "Chairman" (when referring to either sex) is called "chair-one" in NOW. Some groups have adopted "chairperson." "Herstory" is often used when talking about women's contributions. ("One day her-story plus his-story will equal our-story. We will be co-authors"—Wilma Scott Heide.) "Spokesone" is well on its way. The needed revisions are so many that creative word-crafters should get with it, and then start convincing the slow-moving public. It's quite an achievement to get a new word in the dictionary.

Ms. has made it! The twenty-year-old word "Ms." "is being used widely and frequently in respectable publications" as a title for women, said H. B. Woolf, editorial director of Webster-Merriam Dictionaries. "We will most likely enter it in the next edition of our collegiate dictionary." Woolf assumes no responsibility for the addition. "We simply record the language as it is used by educated native speakers."

Which explains what linguistic activism is all about: *consciousness of a few* ⟶ *demands for a new word* ⟶ *increased general consciousness* ⟶ *acceptance of the word as a fact of life.* Legislators in New York and California, among others, are rushing forward with bills to allow women to use the "Ms." designation for voter registration. Women simply made an issue of not having to declare their marital status when men do not. Joke time is over. (But beware of Ms. John Jones!)

Language as weapon. In a town in California, three speakers delivered their remarks at a high-school graduation exercise first in Spanish and then in English. The result was a flap that led a school-board trustee to say, "It was a disgrace to let it happen." Why? Four hundred of the school's five hundred students are Chicanos, and so are their parents. Insisting that English is *the* spoken language is the way the Anglo Establishment maintains second-class status for Chicanos. Asserting one's own speech is central to personhood.

What is repulsive? What is obscene? Our pedestal is supposed to be high enough so that our tender ears are protected from "rough" male language. Like other "protections," this one is used to keep us in our place. "They say they would have to watch their language" is the excuse given to exclude women legislators from the after-hours smoke-filled rooms where the real decisions are made, says Los Angeles assemblywoman Yvonne Brathwaite.

Actually, most of us are less shocked than we are supposed to be. And we're throwing back a few of our own. "Male chauvinist pig" may be repulsive to some women, but who can object to the restrained "m.c.p."?

Battling the linguistic m.c.p.'s. A group of women in Suffolk County, Long Island, took umbrage with the school system for a new alphabet teaching system called Alpha One. Vowels, presented as females, are weak, passive creatures who cannot stand alone, but lean upon the proud, male consonants. The vowels belong to consonants, who choose their favorites. "It presents a very poor image for little girls," said Lois Rodriguez, a kindergarten teacher who refused to use the program.

Since bullets are not our weapons, words take on greater importance. Create them, challenge them, attack them if necessary. Count them—how often do key words appear as opposed to others? For example, "boy" occurs twice as often as "girl" in elementary-school reading matter, according to a recent computerized study. Language is the stuff of struggle. We'll have the last word yet.

If You've Got a Lemon, Make Lemonade

Attune the ear to the way bureaucrats bend the language to their convenience and learn to toss back a few when the situation warrants:

§ *Ghost followers.* A student group planned to meet at the dean's office to talk about more slots for women in the graduate program. Only one showed up at the appointed time. Instead of slinking off in embarrassment, she said, "On behalf of all those who could not be here today . . ."

At a conference where a caucus turned up only two members, one walked up boldly to the mike and said, "It is the position of my contingent that . . ."

§ *Pass the buck.* "If your group is demonstrating and you receive a phone call from a downtown politician asking you to call off your demonstration, tell him 'It's out of my hands; I have no control over that group, because they are so angry,' " says Ellen Lurie in *How to Change the Schools.*

With a little practice we can outwit them, as any woman knows.

25.
ROLE YOUR OWN

A group of fifteen men and women are seated on cushions in the living room of a center for "radical psychiatry" in Berkeley. Several are members of a collective that uses dramatic techniques to help people become more effective in both their personal and wave-making lives, which are seen as interdependent. The rest are participants who are looking for help, or just want a stimulating evening. The atmosphere is warm and supportive.

"I want to work on this problem," volunteers one. "I'm a shop steward. This woman came in with a grievance, and I got all uptight because . . ." "Okay, stop there," says the leader. "Who do you want to play the worker?" The steward and her partner sit in the center and two others "double" for them at their sides. The doubles express what the players are really feeling beneath the surface. ("She's supposed to be my shop steward, but she's not even listening to me . . . she doesn't like me." "Her grievance isn't a real one. It's her own fault . . .") The dialogue goes on for a while, then the two switch roles. Now the group leader encourages feedback from everyone to help the person who brought up the problem understand the underlying dynamics. No "trashing" * is allowed; all comments must be supportive. Painful insights occur, but in a warm, ego-building environment.

That is radical psychiatry's "Role Your Own," a Saturday-night entertainment and enlightenment session. The technique combines creativity and mutual help. By working in a friendly way with the feeling undertow of any gathering, people learn how to support each other. In doing so, we get in better touch with ourselves.

The play spirit is a great plus for women. We play a great many games already—little-girl games, marital games—and all our artifices and pastimes at the heart of "femininity" haven't been notably productive for ourselves or society. But play and creativity are very closely related. Innovative thinkers like Alvin Toffler, the author of *Future Shock,* believe that if the world is to be saved, creative imaginations must be allowed to play the fool, to toy with the absurd. Only later should wild speculation be submitted to harsh critical judgment.

Perhaps all those games we play with our children and each other can be adapted to change society. At least we can make our meetings less dull by inviting the unexpected, the essence of playfulness, such as the great idea that wasn't on the agenda, the surprise action, the joke, or the personal tribute with a light touch. Since so many of us have dabbled in the arts, we could revolutionize tactics. The new woman's style will integrate arts with action—the playful with the serious. Let's give ourselves permission to use all that intuition we're so noted for!

Brainstorming

The Organizer's Manual, prepared by a young activist collective, describes a technique to separate imagination from judgment. The purpose is to withhold evaluation until the maximum number of ideas has been generated.

The leader of the group poses the problem in a way calculated to stimulate thought and permit a wide range of responses. One

* Criticizing destructively.

person should be responsible for jotting down all the ideas that are called out. Brainstormers should note the following:

(1) Criticism is out. Everyone should suspend judgment until evaluation time.

(2) Freewheeling is welcome. The wilder the ideas, the better. Everyone should let her or his imagination soar. It is far easier to tame an idea down than to think one up.

(3) Hitchhiking is invited. Each person is encouraged to ride on, improve on, add to, divide from, and combine with everyone else's ideas.

(4) Quantity is wanted. The more ideas the better. Piling up ideas produces an atmosphere that encourages people to be spontaneous.

The fun of this approach is obvious. By releasing one from that awful question, "But can we really *do* that?" or the even more deadly "Will you head up the committee?", creativity is freed. There is no better way to relieve boredom—or bring new members into a discussion—or maybe even dare to think, "By God, maybe we *could!*"

Rehearsals

Action directed role-play is a must in planning a campaign that involves new or scary tactics. Suppose some women have convinced themselves that they should march into a meeting where a prestigious speaker whom they abhor is holding forth and "take over." The very idea is enough to send shivers down one's spine. But suppose the group has decided that this is a tactic that will work, and the issue is vital enough to risk being obnoxious. How do you plan for such a thing? *Rehearse it.* Have members play the parts of speaker, supporters, interrupters, or outraged member of the audience. Work out the details carefully: Decide who will stand where, and signals for entering and departing. What will you do when and if? The rehearsal will not only generate all kinds of great ideas, but is essential to build the courage that's needed to carry off such an "unfeminine" action.

Role-play the views of the other side before a delegation goes into a lion's den. Suppose it's the management of a company where you are trying to get more women employed. At last you are at the point when you will be sitting across the table. Have someone "double" in the role of personnel manager, speaking his thoughts in a rehearsed negotiation. Discuss. When you are really in the situation, you will be more sure of yourself and less likely to be duped. The same technique works well before visiting congressmen, mayors, and other "public servants."

Civil-rights strategists learned that role-playing was an excellent way to relieve tensions before the action, which otherwise might have led to a blowup at the wrong time. Also, it is a great way to spread the skills, to uncover new talent, and to inject fun into an otherwise heavy campaign. Best of all, the confidence that is so essential to any action is increased. And teamship—you know you can count on each other, and will be laughing together when the ordeal is over.

Games People Should Play

In some racially mixed schools, "simulation games" are used to prepare teachers. School personnel are given a "play" opportunity to meet problems they are likely to face, without experiencing the real-life consequences of their mistakes. These games are more than attitude modifiers. They are offered as learning techniques for institutional change. The purpose is to provoke, to stimulate, and to expose—but in a protected way.

A number of such games that have been produced commercially are both fun and educational. "Blacks & Whites" is a version of Monopoly stacked against the black players, corresponding to stakes in the real world. "Woman & Man" is a variation, exploring sex roles. Both are available through *Psychology Today*. "Sexism," an ingenious game created by the Seattle chapter of NOW, goes further because it forces you into role-play situations and discussion with other players. "When I Grow Up I'm Going to Be Married," a game that shows how time and circumstance affect women, was developed by the State of California Advisory Commission

LIFE IS LIKE A BASEBALL GAME
STRIKE ONE WE'RE POOR
STRIKE TWO, SOME OF US ARE BLACK
STRIKE THREE WE'RE WOMEN
LET'S CALL OFF THE GAME...
..AND MAKE NEW RULES

on the Status of Women. Its purpose is to introduce realism into girls' high-school counseling.

A games program

The Mid-Peninsula YWCA in Palo Alto, California, was struggling with the problem of how to move toward their convention goal: "elimination of racism wherever it exists and by any means necessary." They found themselves playing the wrong kind of games: endless meetings with no action, "feel-good" sessions, "It's the Other Guy," "Ain't It Awful?", and more. So they decided to play games with a point. They wanted to break down their defenses and provide a springboard for action. The hypocrisy that kept women like themselves idle was their central target. They formed the First Priority Players, and now present their game program to as many groups as they can. After the presentation, there is discussion centered on concrete actions to be taken. A conscious effort is made to follow-up on commitments. Sample game:

La Piñata de Justicia Social. A Mexican *piñata,* the traditional candy-filled and decorated papier-mâché pot in fanciful form, dangles from a pole held by one assistant.

> GAME LEADER: Have you ever broken a *piñata?* It's a lovely custom. But picture the *piñata* as a beautiful package of goodies just out of reach of Spanish-speaking people. Blindfolded by an alien culture (puts blindfold around player), made dizzy by false promises (turns player around), then told to whack away at the goodies, while the power that holds the rope yanks them away when they get too close (goes through motions). As an individual they don't have much chance, but together . . . you have *La Raza.* That's how we'll play it now. For each blow for social justice that you can suggest, there will be one whack at the *piñata.*

Sample blows include: Bi-lingual classes. Special education program for migrant families. Health clinic. Buy union lettuce. More Spanish-speaking teachers. Register Chicano and Puerto Rican voters. Housing program for migrants. When at last the *piñata* breaks, the candies are shared by all. To close, the game leader cries, *"Viva la piñata de Justicia Social,"* the audience,

"Viva." Game leader: *"Viva la piñata." "Viva."* This is repeated until everyone *feels* it.

The games program ("guaranteed to leave you uplifted, upended, and uptight") made it possible for the group to: (1) discuss issues before organizations that would not have considered a straight speaker on the subject, (2) expose the negative game-playing on controversial subjects that is so characteristic of these organizations, and (3) recruit people to specific actions. Most important, the participants themselves absorbed the lessons.

Walk a mile in my shoes

If experience is the best teacher, many of us are quite disadvantaged, We, or those we are trying to convince, may need some remedial studies. The kind of learning that you can't find in books is the most valuable of all, because human beings make the greatest strides when they feel hunger, fear, oppression, hate, violence, condescension.

Once, when I was a volunteer coordinator for a ghetto poverty program, a young white man wanted to "become involved." The night before he had been in the center of a racial disturbance; his car was stoned, and angry blacks spat upon him. He said his first reaction was fury, and only later did he think, "This is how blacks feel." Until that experience he had felt no responsibility. Now he identified with those on the receiving end of racial hate.

Some of these switches occur unintentionally. You don't plan them, but you can help to pin down the lessons learned and translate them into action.

§ Two staunch Republicans were hopping mad after they accepted an "invitation" to witness a "riot" and ended up being arrested for what they believed was an act of good citizenship. Young people had expressed their determination to "confront the establishment" by continuing a rock concert after the 11 P.M. curfew. Merchants invited responsible citizens to attend and witness the lawlessness. The Republicans who answered the call and listened to the concert were arrested along with long-haired youths and a sixty-nine-year-old woman, and spent the night in jail. "Up until Saturday night I was one hundred per cent behind the administration," said one. "I thought things like we must have a reason for being in Vietnam. But after seeing the cops and the kids, now I'm not so sure."

Some are carefully planned as a learning experience:

§ Twenty-three shocked trial judges emerged from a night in Nevada State Prison appalled by the episode. They had volunteered as part of a seminar for judges. "After that experience I'm going to work for total reform of our prisons," said one. "I was in a cage like an animal," "They should take two bulldozers out there and tear it down," were other comments.

§ "How many of us arrogant world-shapers *knew* hunger? Could we learn it and teach it at the same time?" The hunger show, called Liferaft Earth, was an attempt to do so. Organized by the staff of Whole Earth Catalog in October 1969, it was designed as a game, attempting to make very personal the matter of population control. A parking lot in Hayward, California, was the scene.

The rules were announced in advance: A lot of people would stay publicly together for a week without eating. Anybody could leave at any time, but could not return, their departure being considered a death. "The bait for the media, besides the noble cause, was suspense. Who would come to the event? How many would last the week? Who would they be? What kind of stuff would go on with hungry people penned up together?" Who survived the week? Fifty-two, "the hairiest and the quietest . . . lots of girls." All of this is described in *The Last Whole Earth Catalog,* which also has a rental film of the event and suggestions for similar strategies of game change.

§ "Welfare Monopoly" was a game thought up by the Christian Conscience Committee of the Berea Presbyterian Church in St. Louis. One hundred twenty families, including twenty-one state legislators, agreed to go on a welfare allotment (which provided eleven cents a meal per person) for one week. In addition, they were mailed "Chance" and "Community Chest" cards, which either caused extra hardship or provided a benefit. Players recorded as "stolen" any food consumed over the eleven-cent limit. Women actually on welfare, who served as telephone "caseworkers," turned on the frustration from their own experience, offering such advice as "try the Salvation Army" at times when that office was closed. Meanwhile, the real welfare office was picketed.

Some experiences are planned for a different purpose, but provide firsthand learning as a side benefit.

§ *"Operation Open City,"* the housing program of the New York Urban League, uses one hundred fifty white volunteers, mostly women, to check out cases of suspected discrimination in housing. When a complaint is made, a volunteer who takes on the characteristics of the person rejected (income, family status, and desired accommodations) applies for the housing. When she signs the lease, an investigator from the New York Commission on Human Rights moves in. A volunteer commented that what had been a relatively remote problem that bothered her conscience had become one of personal involvement once she had witnessed some "screaming bigots."

Some firsthand research assignments can be encouraged by any group engaged in social action. Devise them to fit your issue. Examples:

§ Sit in a waiting room of the maternity ward of a hospital where welfare cases are placed. Strike up some conversations.

§ Next picking season, do a day's work in the fields. Talk with migrant workers.

§ Turn off the heat in winter and spend one night in a cold house.

§ Make the rounds one day with a visiting nurse, or a home-school coordinator.

§ Go to a park where elderly people sit. How are things going? What are their problems?

§ Use only recycled items for a period. How does it affect your lifestyle?

§ Call City Hall with a complaint that your landlord did not give heat, or the toilet is not working.

§ For men who want to know what it feels like to be a woman, Redstockings of San Francisco suggests: Wear a woman's liberation button publicly. Allow yourself to be treated like a woman by other men.

Zaps

A zap, according to *The Organizer's Manual,* is symbolic shock therapy aimed at the status quo. A zap pits irrationality against hardened rationality. It can be humorous in content but deadly serious in intent. Anyone who comes into viewing, hearing, smelling, tasting, or feeling distance can be zapped.

There is nothing further from the style of a middle-class-female-over-thirty organization than this psychological warfare of the young against the establishment. Would *you* mail roaches to a slum landlord? Send dirt back along with bills to a polluter? Spread zap graffiti around? However, just because such unladylike tactics are so unexpected, they could be potent weapons. Use them with caution, or they will turn off the very women you wish to organize, more than demoralize the opposition. Consider the mythical burning bra, the zap that never came off. "*I'm* not a bra burner" became another kind of battle cry.

Effective zaps

§ The Detroit chapter of the National Organization for Women held a news conference in the city morgue to point up deaths from abortion.

§ During congressional hearings on school-lunch–program appropriations, a group of hungry-looking children watching legislators eat was an appropriate zap in the tradition of Mother Jones.

"Zap FAP" is the Welfare Rights Organization's slogan to defeat Nixon's Family Assistance Program, which they consider completely inadequate for family needs. The low-income women that comprise this action group have little fear of zaps in either word or deed.

Guerrilla Theater

Real guerrilla theater is theater of the streets, performed for political or social impact, usually before a chance audience of passersby. Anyone interested should read the specific literature on the subject or, better yet, contact a performing group. However, a great number of organizations will at one time or another wish to stage an action with dramatic impact, symbolic gesture strong enough to break through accepted myths to the reality below the surface. Don't hesitate to do so because you don't have a performing troupe. Dramatic actions are good for the performers, good for the audience, and great for publicity.

§ PANG (People Against Nerve Gas) organized an effective multifaceted and succssful campaign against the transportation of this deadly substance across the state of Washington. The climax of the struggle came when well-dressed citizens in the downtown shopping area fell "dead" in the streets, "overcome" by fumes, to stimulate possible effects of an accidental leakage.

§ At a workshop in Seattle, Saul Alinsky suggested to an organizer of people on old-age assistance fighting cuts in their allotments that her group set up tables outside a restaurant where legislators dined. With meager brown-bag lunches they would have a picnic, going past the feasting legislators in the restaurants to use the toilets.

Props and Costumes

The use of accessories comes very naturally. Here's another way to put our latent talent, and our traditions to good use.

§ Women from Women's International League for Peace and Freedom (WILPF) in Palo Alto made attractive butcher-boy aprons with PAX appliquéd front and back. They wore these sandwich boards as they distributed leaflets weekly in their Don't-buy-from-war-contractors campaign. The aprons made them stand out from the crowd, and provided a handy place to store extra leaflets.

§ Leafletters in a boycott aimed at increasing employment of minorities stenciled red, white, and blue "All-American Hiring" designs on shopping bags.

§ A YWCA wished to dramatize the plight of Mexican-Americans who were calling for politically viable legislative districts in California's reapportionment plans. The Y women demonstrated their point with pumpkin pies, which they smeared over with Rediwhip ("white goo") until the brown pie was completely obliterated. The stunt was fun, and received considerable publicity.

§ NOW women demonstrating for the Equal Rights Amendment on August 26 (the anniversary of women's suffrage) wore dresses recalling the early feminists. Other costumes and props included women chained to typewriter, a cap-and-gown–clad woman carrying pail and mop, a male "bunny," and other visual images aimed at the press and designed to dispel womanhood myths.

When planning an action, think: Is there any prop or costume that would enliven this event?

Visual Aids

Remember the chalk talks that used to be popular on TV? If you can recruit or train (encourage) someone to do that, there will be no difficulty in getting an audience. Flip boards used to be effective as an adjunct to soap-box oratory. They were a series of cartoons or charts, poster size, set up on an easel. As the speakers talked they flipped over a page, creating suspense as the audience anticipated the next picture. A cranky is a new version, a series of pictures drawn on a roll of paper and cranked from right to left. Feminists use this delightful device to put "her" into history.

Try collage at a small-group meeting. Bring lots of old magazines, scissors, and rubber cement. Have a theme for the collage ("What is a woman?") or leave it open. Discuss the results—what it meant to the person who created the collage, and what others saw.

Of course, there are innumerable film strips, as well as professional and semiprovisional aids of all kinds, that a little research can uncover. But if you have talent in your group, use it by all means. Then work toward making the idea or product available outside your group. A good gimmick can turn into a fund-raising item.

Most groups have at least one camera bug. Use that skill for displays, for publicity pictures, for the record incorporated in a scrapbook. McLuhanize the tired leaflets and speeches with the visual image, while perhaps starting someone on a new career.

§ "Ecology freaks" set up display boards in a shopping center with photos contrasting natural beauty with the horrors of unimpeded development. Local shots gave emphasis to a petition to change zoning rules.

§ A NOW member working to change sex tracking in public schools photographed an elementary playground. She caught the graffiti and "apartheid" play of boys and girls, then made slides from textbooks that promote separate roles for men and women. She divided all this into a slide show for PTAs and school personnel. Not only were these groups more willing to book the program than a mere speaker, but the message was far more effectively presented.

"Role your own" thing. There's no reason why we can't find self-fulfillment and blast the establishment at the same time. Play the fool, toy with the absurd, make a game of it—laugh! Then pie in their kissers!

26.
MONEY (I): ITS DANGERS AND HOW TO GET IT

Who pays the piper calls the tune. At least the musicians will be careful to play the donor's favorites and avoid songs he detests. Unfortunately, money with no strings attached is a beautiful dream. There is no such thing, because even if the givers have no intention of laying down conditions, there are always questions

Bread.

FAT CAT
FOUNDATION
NOO
FUND
RAISING
NO
FUND
RAISING
MR. BIG BREAD
FUND
RAISING
PENCILS
FUND
RAISING

floating around in the air: "Do you think *they* [the donor] would approve?" "Next time we ask, will they hold this against us?" "We might lose our tax-deductible status if we do that." A donor—government agency, foundation, or individual—becomes a ghost at every meeting. Furthermore, the IRS number (conferred on an organization by the Internal Revenue Service to permit donors to take tax deductions) can be revoked at any time a group steps beyond the bonds of charity and education.

Moreover money is not so easy to get as is generally assumed, if you are not a large and established organization. Even then, fund raising can become a major part of the program. Wave-making efforts don't fall into tax-deductible categories, either. People who want change are not received with the universal approval, and on the contrary are usually rewarded with unfavorable publicity for their efforts. In other words, the more you stir things up, the harder it is to get financing.

Add to this the competition for the few exceptions to that rule. When it comes to funding, organizations become loners, all scrambling for the crumbs from the master's table. Each group looks at its potential allies as rivals for the coveted dollar, guarding its donor list and eyeing with suspicion any other group approaching its turf. Much of the hard feeling between organizations that overlap stems from competition for funds. Doling out a few dollars here, withholding them there, is an effective divide-and-conquer technique employed by those in power.

If this is not enough to discourage you, consider the bad effects of money when you do get it. If you are able to pay a salary, staff are separated from volunteers, with inevitable problems. Either the volunteers slack up on the assumption that the staff should carry on, or paid personnel become career-oriented, with personal motivations overriding the goals of the organization. Or, having established responsibility for a salary, the group is diverted from its original goal to the maintenance of that office and staff. Then there's the real danger that your leaders, seduced by their new professional status, will be co-opted into a mild reform program. Money is not only the root of the evil, it is also the stalk and the branch.

If you don't really need money, do without it. If the project can be carried forward on voluntary effort alone, so much the better. Breakaway, a "free university" for women in Berkeley, conducts over thirty courses a semester for three hundred women without even a budget. A registration fee of one dollar covers the cost of a brochure and meeting place for registration. Everything else is free. Leaders charge nothing, and classes are held in homes.

All over the country there are innovative projects existing on a hand-to-mouth basis, many intentionally. Money is collected when continued operation is threatened, which adds to the cliff-hanging excitement. "Trust in God—She will provide" is the prevailing mood.

Because the majority of us have been mentally removed from the marketplace, we are reluctant to ask others for money, at least for larger sums. The assertiveness and salesmanship required for successful fund raising is repugnant to many. Even though we have spent countless hours begging for every good cause and charity that ever was invented, on the whole these efforts have been largely unproductive, if you consider the woman hours expended.

Ask any professional fund raiser. They will tell you that in any large campaign, 80 percent of the funds comes from 20 percent of the donors, with the mass of donors contributing only 20 percent. The pros spend their major time where the big money is, but recognize that the large-scale promotion and organization necessary to collect many small donations is an essential adjunct. Women volunteers do most of that grass-roots collection, which in turn provides the public support and prestige that paves the way for an approach to the foundation, corporation, or large donor. And of course even the small donations add to the total.

From a feminist point of view, it's one big rip-off. The woman is conned into thinking that she is performing an essential service (and of course she is for the fund raiser), but it is part of the familiar volunteer syndrome that extends woman's homemaker role to encompass all community ills. And even her work as a fund collector is mere window dressing for the real action, which transpires in a man's world. No wonder women are turned off from fund raising!

But consider our grandmothers. In the early 1850s, when Susan B. Anthony was first organizing women's clubs in the state of New York, she came head-on with the dilemma. Women's lodges formed after an earlier speech-making tour had fallen apart one year later. One reason, she decided, was that women had no money of their own. If they worked, their wages belonged to their husbands. If they did not work, they were lucky to receive what was literally pin money.

The early feminists battled a decade to win the right to property. Over the years the old English common law that regarded women as perpetually dependent minors fell state by state under their untiring onslaught. Each of those campaigns required money—for travel, for printed materials, for legal briefs and more. But women had no funds of their own. How did Susan B. Anthony raise money? *She asked for it,* because she knew it was necessary for what had to be done. She sold tracts, passed the basket, sought out male supporters, and incorporated fund raising into every activity. *If our grandmothers could do it despite all the obstacles, psychological as well as physical, who are we to say that we can't raise money?*

Money is the soft underbelly of the beast. We must have it to co-opt the system in any sustained way, or to set up alternative structures, and to conduct mind-changing on a mass scale. One deciding factor is size. The larger the organization, the more it needs paid staff, just to keep communications open.

Another factor is time. A short-range campaign can often do extremely well on enthusiasm and hat-passing alone, but a long-range goal needs a wider funding base.

Important questions to ask: Can we combine our fund raising with our issues so that we will be educating as we collect money? Can we win new members in the process of our fund drive? Will our organization be stronger when we finish?

If you decide to make the plunge, work to overcome the hang-ups. To secure that money, take on some of the characteristics of the system that many deplore. Learn to think *money,* just as we're learning to think *law*. Become capable saleswomen and learn public relations. Be convinced of your cause that you have no compunction to ask anyone to support it. God (or the professional fund raiser) may provide the contacts, but you will have to make the pitch.

Fund Raising as the Pros Do It

Here are some rules of thumb recommended by a professional fund raiser:

—Fund raising is getting organized to ask people for money. You can't get off the hook by saying you'll hire a professional to do the job for you. Fund raisers are consultants who will help you decide how to do it, but you will still be the ones asking for the money.

—Have a plan, as long range as possible. You should have a six-month goal, a one-year goal, and a five-year goal. Planning is a key to fund raising.

—Get the membership involved. Set financial goals and quotas. Members should be thoroughly convinced of why they are giving and why they are asking others to give.

—Study your strengths and your weaknesses. What do you have to sell? What services could you perform?

—Fund raising should be from varied sources: membership, fund drive, products, events. Sometimes grants as well.

—Having a calendar for everything. Allow yourself enough time to prepare, but not too much.

—Don't ask, "How much would you like to give?" Say, "We hoped you might donate $—." Challenge people to give. Always ask for more than you expect.

—Saturate the community with information about your project and organization. Publicity sets the stage.

—Go after the big money first. Spend most time on larger donors. Fifty percent of funds should already be in before a mass campaign.

—Issue progress reports.

—In appeal materials, include letters and quotes from people with clout. Draft what you want said and take it to the person you want to sign it.

—Use what you can: influence, intimidation, favors, friendship, and other leverage. People give because people they know ask them.

—Pledge cards will bring you greater commitments. They provide the donor with more flexibility in regard to taxes, and a chance to spread the donation over a longer time. Also, it keeps communication open.

—Ask for larger gifts in person. Know your subject well and keep talking. Aggressive selling is the hallmark of a good fund raiser.

—Get "big" people to head the campaign. Put capable people in second positions. Invade the power structure.

—Don't skimp on expenses, but don't be lavish either. Use first-class postage.

—Be sure that *everyone* is thanked: the campaigner, donor, helper. Thank the person who said "no" but listened.

Thirty-five Ways to Raise Money

Starting with devices we're already familiar with, we can think up new forms of fund raising, or old forms with a twist. These should educate as well as replenish the bank account, help bring in new members, utilize the creativity of the group, and be fun rather than a drag.

(1) *Recycled-fashion show.* Old clothes modeled with all the zing of Paris. Commentary could include your ecological points in a light satirical tone. Might combine with an old-clothes rummage sale dressed up as Carnaby Street.

(2) *How-to booklets.* Poor woman's guide to your area (services, people to call, good-'n'-cheap restaurants, shops, rip-offs to avoid, etc.). How to beat Christmas. Ecology trips. Whatever else is useful and you would like to share.

(3) *Cards, notepaper.* Produce your own, or buy in bulk from a national organization in your orbit.

(4) *Counter-gift shop.* A coalition of peace organizations runs a Dove Store in Palo Alto, California, selling crafts on consignment, cards and stationery, as well as providing a meeting place and headquarters. A woman's center could pay for its facilities by a well-organized shop of this kind.

(5) *Boutique.* Variation of above. Sell on consignment, or products of a collective. Jewelry, candles, macramé, quilts, dresses, and crochet. Has to be promoted and advertised, however.

(6) *Recycle shop.* Used items, how-to-do materials, information and classes on repairs.

(7) *Patents.* Women invent lots of things but seldom patent them. A patent center to assist women in finding out commercial possibilities of their devices could split profits between the inventor and the sponsoring group.

(8) *Classes.* Most women may be poor, but manage to pay for what they want. Subjects with personal appeal: Women and the Law, Writing for Women's Magazines, Making the Most of Your Assets, New Career Potential for Mature Women—all will draw participants, if they are well-publicized and well-taught. Charge the going rate for such a course, asking those who can to contribute to scholarships for those who can't. Teachers? Many persons would rather donate their time to your organization than money.

(9) *Cocktail party with a twist.* Anything unusual enough will raise money because people will attend out of curiosity. The invitation should startle. "Name" guests could be the draw. New York NOW raised $1,400 at one such party.

(10) *Poppas and Mommas.* NOW suggests a temporary or weekend childcare station in a shopping center where shoppers can leave children for short periods. Males, as well as females, should staff the center. Hand out materials on childcare. Encourage local merchants to contribute, considering the benefits to their sales.

(11) *Nonevent.* A nonannual dinner asking for the donation of price for the tickets. A nonbake sale for alternative-school fund raising might invite participants to eat their own cake and send you the frosting—green, of course.

(12) *No-talent show.* But lots of participational stuff that will prove the contrary. Improvisational-theater people can sometimes draw an audience in with great results. Have a bar for extra dollars, and more uninhibited talent.

(13) *Make-your-own.* Antique wreath, centerpiece, flower arrangement, quilt, collage, junk art. Several activities going on at once will attract more people.

(14) *Paid-for-a-day*. Charge your husband at least a minimum hourly wage for your homemaking services to make a contribution to your special cause.

(15) *Men's potluck*. Let them compete or cooperate with each other. Should be a conversation stimulator as well as a good fund raiser.

(16) *Walk-a-thon* for ecology. Solicit sponsors to contribute according to miles walked. (Must be tax-deductible.) Lends itself to broad support and good publicity.

(17) *Book autographing*. Also records. The celebrity's presence will bring people to whom you can make a direct-funds appeal. Or a profit-sharing arrangement can be made with the celebrity—or both.

(18) *Forum*. Charge. A reasonable admission will not keep an audience away. On the contrary: sometimes it is better to rent a hall than use a free one where you cannot charge or take a collection.

(19) *Everybody's birthday party*. A really lively party with everyone bringing gifts to the organization—in kind or in cash. Read the birthday cards.

(20) *Your birthday gift*. Ask each member to make a gift on their birthday, in gratitude for having made it through another year. Especially suitable for ecology groups.

(21) *Flea market or garage sale*. Try a reverse sales approach. "Do you really need one? We decided to get rid of ours." "Uses too much electricity." "Just another thing to dust." As they leave, ask for a donation of all the money they have saved.

(22) *Organic-garden party*. Demonstrations of gardening and cooking the organic way. Sale of products and materials to do it.

(23) *Organic food and homemade wine tasting party*.

(24) *Simple-fare fair*. Antiplastic alternatives to the "good life." Lots of participational things. Displays.

(25) *Environmental charter flight*. With ecologist guide to point out the good and bad examples of regional land use. The charge might just cover expenses, but provide a preliminary to individual requests for funds later.

(26) *Tours*. Ecological, planning, poverty, and urban problems. Very useful as an educational introduction with direct fund raising to follow.

(27) *Holiday counterevents.* Anticonsumerism Christmas. Feminist's Mother's Day with a new appreciation of mothers, past and present. Peace Memorial Day.

(28) *Small business.* Make it fit the cause: bicycle repair shop for ecologists, auto repair for feminists, print shop for coalition.

(29) *Movie benefit.* Locate the films that relate to your issue, preferably that also entertain or move people. A film series is not much more work. Popcorn or drinks will add to the intake.

(30) *Theater party.* Buy out the house for one performance of an appropriate play. Or bring a performing group to you.

(31) *Run a radio station for a day.* Solicit donations or gifts in kind.

(32) *"Remember when" night.* Good for the older members' morale, and can provide historical perspective on any issue: feminist, environmental, or peace. Can be done with slides, skits, speakers. Also music and dances of an earlier period.

(33) *Welfare lunch.* Serve beans, rice, and other surplus-foods, charging full price. (The Welfare Rights Organization held a Salute to the Poor, with a meal costing fourteen cents—the price allotted to each person per meal on Family Assistance Program.)

(34) *Prison lunch.* Variation of above in order to make more realistic a discussion of prison reform.

(35) Make up a case of *items for sale* with your logo or slogan: balloons, T-shirts, posters, cards, stationery, bumper strips, buttons. Secure portable table. Ask permission to set up your wares at all large gatherings that other groups organize.

Putting It On

Before deciding on a project, go to the library and get out a book with at least a hundred fund-raising ideas. Choose some that could be original and get your message across at the same time. Now try these out at a brainstorming session, letting imaginations go. Then determine which is the most feasible, profitable, and educational. Work out a plan and schedule. Involve as many people as possible, especially newcomers. Keep records, evaluate your results, and be sure to thank everyone.

Elements of a fund-raising campaign

Take an imaginary group: a Women's Legal Center in a large city with a law school. It is a loose organization of deeply committed women lawyers, law students, feminists, and friends who have been carrying a heavy load of activities, legal and educational. The excitement and demands of the Women's Movement have pulled them in many directions. They are at a point where they are terribly frustrated for lack of money. There are all kinds of things to be done, but none of them possible without funding. At last they have reached the conclusion that it would be worth sacrificing their looseness and independence for a firm financial base. What do they do now?

(1) They incorporate and form a nonprofit organization in order to apply for Internal Revenue Service tax-deductible status. (Check this out with a lawyer. Expect considerable delay.)

(2) They extend their list of incorporators to a sizeable Board of Directors. The board would be representative of varied segments of the community sympathetic to their purpose. It would include status persons—those with contacts in moneyed circles—as well as women who know the severest problems firsthand. By-laws are formulated.

(3) Goals are outlined: carry through test cases on special interest of women; train women to become lay advocates in interests of women, such as welfare proceedings, divorce, and ecology; work with women's groups interested in legislative reforms to assist in drafting of legislation; sponsor classes and workshops on legal problems of women.

(4) Immediate goal: Raise a fund sufficient to launch the project and lay the basis for long-range foundation and other funding. A realistic goal of $50,000 is set. Four months are allocated.

(5) A volunteer fund raiser is located who will work for expenses, and will train others in fund raising. Leadership is lined up: a campaign chairman and a cabinet. All board members are involved.

(6) Subcommittees include: *foundations committee*—studies local and national possibilities, and draws up proposals; *public*

relations—starts immediately with publicity campaign, calls press conference, arranges for interviews and TV appearances and plans open house; *speakers' bureau*—solicits speaking opportunities. All speakers stress what the organization will do with the money; *individual-donors committee*—each one enlists three other persons to either call upon other prospects or have a fund-raising event. Special attention to lawyers, law faculty, and their wives. (They contribute themselves before soliciting others: "You can't sell what you won't buy."); *prospect-lists committee*—the entire board is involved in compiling a list of people to be visited personally, and a general list. They use directories, ask people in other organizations, and collect friends and contacts from their own group.

(7) A calendar is drawn up, including:

—Open house.

—Visits to major donors, preceded by role-play sessions. (Leadership, in pairs, visit the best prospects.)

—Campaign kick-off forum. Speakers, pledges.

—Work party to get off a general fund-appeal mailing.

—Publicity events. Cabinet meetings. Progress reports. Board meetings.

—Campaign closing—celebration theater party.

—Evaluation session.

—Long-range funding plan finalized: foundation proposals, memorial-gifts plan.

WARNING: The above is by no means a blueprint, or a how-to-do-it plan. The outline is given to indicate the direction a sophisticated fund-raising program might go. There is more to it than that. Locate your friendly local fund raiser and talk it over.

27.
MONEY (II): GRANTSWOMANSHIP

"While you are up, get me a grant," used to be the joke in those circles that read all the guidelines and foundation reports. Unfortunately, those days are gone, perhaps forever. For one thing, the circle has widened, and competition for the lush subsidy is fierce. For every grant that is made, hundreds of proposals are turned down. Besides, the field has become highly professionalized, with bureaus in every major institution with no other responsibilities than seeking government and private funding. Consultive services have multiplied to research the prospects, and associations formed with the avowed function of grantsmanship. You provide the project and the qualifications; they assist in proposal writing and selling, for a fee or a percentage.

There are two sources of grants: the public sector and the private. In general, the government is the more difficult to deal with in terms of specifications, guidelines, reports, and all manner of strings. Even what appears to be a clear-cut proposal that falls right into the purpose of funding usually entails an incredible amount of hassle and endless delay. On the other hand, that's where the money is, and those of us who believe in the absolute necessity of our projects cannot turn up our noses and walk away. It is one thing, for example, to call for twenty-four-hour childcare under parental control, and quite another to endure the battles that will ensue after appropriations are at last made.

The government (all branches) is susceptible to pressure, and therein lies both the problem and the solution. Demands, organization, and action produce funds; demands, organization, and action by the opposition tie up funds with impossible restrictions. The only out is more pressure. Like housework, it's never-ending. You think you have the place cleaned up, and there it is all dirty again. The only way to work for government funding is to have no illusions, be as cynical as your fellow manipulators, and have a strong stomach.

Foundation grant hunting is somewhat better. However, the money there is usually earmarked for limited purposes. Generally foundations consider their funds as seed money. Continuing commitments are not popular. The more influential ones like to think of themselves as society's cutting edge, pioneering pilot projects and research in advance of government or community support. The point of view of the directors determines the thrust of that edge.

A foundation directory, available at most libraries, lists alphabetically by state the names, addresses, and other pertinent information of 6,803 foundations, although even this is not a complete list. The Foundation Library Center in New York, and smaller ones elsewhere, provide a setting for the dreary research that has to be undertaken to develop grantswomanship.

One point this information will not mention is that it is *who you know* that is the most important determinant of all. Professional consultants are most concerned with possible connections board members might have with foundation directors. Romula R. Soldevilla, director of Institutional Fundraising, Inc. (a professional fund-raising agency), says, "Every foundation that you are going to apply to will also have received at the same time applications from other people who want money. . . . Among these other people there will be friends of the foundation board and it is those proposals that are going to get first consideration. Now wouldn't you like that advantage?"

Of course you would, but suppose you check all your adherents for contacts with the donors and you come up with a blank. In that case you have to create them, or employ other tactics. Use ingenuity to get an appointment to talk about your proposal face to face with a director of the foundation, if possible, or at least with a staff person. Then sell. Foundation people (men) are as vulnerable as anyone else to the contradictions of the system. They may want to be innovative, to follow the fashion of philanthropy, susceptible to guilt, anxious to prove how liberal (broad-minded, non-sexist, unprejudiced, advanced) they are, or open to tokenism. Some are genuinely forward-looking. Whatever is the case, psych it out and drive your points home.

If we can overcome our hang-ups and dive into the funding scene we will learn a great many things about how the system works. While we finance our projects, we will:

—find that developing grant proposals can be an organizing tool. Just writing it up forces us to clear up the fuzziness. What do we really want to accomplish? How can we go about it? What will it cost? Who will do it?

—develop skills that are necessary to bring our good programs to fruition.

—learn how to take care of business.

Financial Actions

Stockholder actions

Corporations make large donations that are tax-deductible from profits. Social-minded proxy groups are fighting for greater human commitment, and industry is beginning to react defensively to the pressure. NOW's Stockholder Action Task Force is urging women who own stock to exercise their right to attend annual meetings, put forth shareholder resolutions, vote their shares, inspect records of the corporation, and even bring suit where the directors have acted to injure the corporation.

Selective benevolence

In making your own gifts, choose *only* those that really reflect your viewpoint. In refusing others, make your reasons known. For example, a feminist writes, "I am most surely in support of your goals. However, in looking over the names of your executive committee, and Board of Directors, I find that you have no women as officers, and only one woman on the Board. I cannot contribute to a project which holds the opinions and expertise of women to be of so little value." More of these letters will put more of us on the inside.

Foundation accountability

Tax exemption is conferred upon foundations by the people, who in effect pick up the tab by paying heavier taxes. Yet reporting requirements are very lax. If foundations had to report more fully, they would be more susceptible to pressure, and their giving would be liberalized. Citizen/consumer investigations are overdue.

Socially conscious mutual funds

Pax World Fund, started under the auspices of the United Methodist Church, will not invest in any company that does more than five percent of its business in war-related industries. The Dreyfus Third Century Fund limits its investments to those contributing to "the quality of life for all Americans." The Social Dimensions Fund is interested only in companies with "intrinsic social value," such as pollution-control equipment and educational materials, and "whose actions enhance the well-being of employees, consumers and communities." They will have a limited portfolio.

Bequests and memorials

This is one area where we can have real impact. It is a myth that women, because we outlive our husbands, control all the wealth. Widows may own large assets, but these are usually controlled by male relatives or financial advisers. As women are becoming more independent, however, we will be responsive to bequests to environmental, peace, and feminist programs. Some action organizations have tax-deductible arms, which could be included in many women's wills, especially by women who remember the suffrage struggle. For those of us who see our mothers or grandmothers in a new light, consider a memorial gift in their names to such programs. How better to insure the continuity of the Women's Movement than to leave behind a new foundation dedicated to its continuance—a practical form of immortality!

The starting place for fund raising is self-interest. When you realize that the differential between the earnings of an average woman who works full time and an average man, figured out over a 40-year working period, comes to $64,230, job equality quite literally becomes a sixty-four-thousand-dollar question. Childcare, for a woman who goes back to work or school, costs up to $2,000 per year. Tax inequalities add up to a sizable figure for many women. Changing these inequities means money in the bank, and is well worth an investment of time and cash, even in the monetary sense.

Beyond the porkchops are the human questions—and our input into the great issues of the day. Unfortunately, freedom not only is not free, you can't even get it wholesale. You have to pay the full price.

28.
Toward a Positive New Woman's Style

"Positive" has so many negative connotations that it is almost a dirty word. A positive person is a Pollyanna—simple-minded—has illusions—is naïve—doesn't understand the way things really are—is a reformist, accommodationist, or worse. People in the know carefully steer away from appearing too positive. It is fashionable to see the enormity of the problems and the uncontested strength of the adversary. But only a fraction of those who bemoan the circumstances lift a finger to change them.

It's time to take a closer look at that word "positive," dust it off, and see if it doesn't really fit what we're all about. There is nothing more positive than sisterhood. Assertiveness rather than passivity is the essence of the new feminism. Action, as contrasted with do-nothingness, is the way we're going, if we're going anywhere. Without hope, there will be no action, which requires us to overcome despair.

In the new Woman's Movement there are valiant attempts to forge a new positive style. The small groups especially are attempting to develop mutual support on a deeper level than in most organizations, as they sort out the blocks that have prevented us from accepting each other and ourselves. "We are all women—we have all felt the effects of sexism" is a strong unifying bond that overcomes age differences and personal interests.

When we turn outward to tackle the social ills, the bonds break down. Why? One reason is that, in reaction against hierarchies, power trips, and number-oneness, new strictures are laid down that make action difficult. No one can move until everyone is ready to move and at the same pace.

On the opposite pole are the by-law enthusiasts who believe that any organizational problem can be solved with a new rule. Order is essential, but laws are singularly ineffective in organizational work, especially with women. We do things because we want to. As soon as we have to, the fun is gone.

Another problem is perfectionism. There is reluctance to risk any serious involvement until all the kinks, personal or group, are worked out. Unfortunately, we have a great number of kinks. And, let's face it, it's hard to like everybody you have to work with. Charlie Brown loves humanity. It's just people he can't stand. Sisterhood is great too—but the sisters are hard to take some of the time. Maybe when we've built that brave new world that is free of sexism, racism, war, and inhumanity, we'll all shape up. Meanwhile, we can draw strength from Susan B. Anthony and her sisters and get on with it.

Some Elements of the New Style

Hope without illusions

The discouraged person is the one who has been disillusioned. To avoid that, consciously and continually discard illusions. Reality is the only way to go. The new style will encourage others to accept reality as the starting point, always with the belief that it can be changed for the better. Begin where the world is, not where you would like it to be.

Collectivity

Whatever form of organization, new or old, hierarchical or co-operative, work to build a collective spirt. Leadership is not incompatible with a collective.

Respect individuals

Accept people as they are, moving *with* their strong points, *around* their weaknesses.

Respect varied lifestyles

Without respect for self, there can be no respect for others. (That includes middle-class white women, even those over thirty.) If we believe in the concept of more choices for women, that implies a willingness to accept a whole variety of styles, even those that go against the grain. The new style will be open to a wider spectrum.

Balance

There are always twin dangers. You can move too slowly, for fear of losing someone, fear of controversy, or fear of what outsiders might say—or you can move too fast, by plowing right over the feelings of the majority. The new style will strive to achieve a working balance. Questions that must be faced will not be avoided, based on understanding "where the membership is" on any controversial issue. A balanced style recognizes that collectivity can be built only on compromise.

Be an optimist

Is the glass half full or half empty? You can't organize a half-empty glass. You can expose it, deplore it, and bemoan the fact that soon the rest will be gone. But to organize you start with what is. That eliminates mirages, too. It does not help to say the glass is nearly full when there are only a few drops left. Say—the glass has one ounce in it already, and go on from there.

Alliances Coalitions Conferences

Maybe if we were driving, this thing wouldn't be in reverse.

29.
FINDING COMMON GROUND

You are working for a bill to give cease-and-desist powers (teeth) to the Equal Employment Opportunities Commission (EEOC). It is stalled in Congress. Do you:

• wait? (After all, they'll get to it in time.)

• forget the EEOC? (That's an establishment agency, anyway.)

• make a list of all organizations interested in a stronger EEOC; call an informal exploratory meeting to discuss "how can we get the bill calendared?"

You have been working for a childcare bill. It passes Congress at last, but is vetoed. Do you:

• give up?

• decide to move to Sweden?

• phone people you know in other organizations that worked for the measure and call a joint press conference fast to urge Congress to override the veto, or work toward next year's bill?

You read in the paper that the government has just trimmed the rolls of children eligible for the free-lunch program. Sounds bad. You call the local welfare rights organization and learn they are incensed. The church food-for-the-poor leader doesn't like it, and a school administrator thinks it will be impossible to administer. Do you:

• say, "Ain't it awful?"

• put your kids in private schools so they won't have to share their sandwiches?

• suggest to all the others a jointly sponsored public forum on "How hungry should a child be to get a free lunch?"

You have attended a conference on pollution, and you have been told at length by "experts" that you are the key to a clean environment (by buying low-lead gasoline, saving tin cans, and recycling bags). You also learn how poorly even the weakest laws are enforced. Do you:

• go home and determine to do your part? (You'll take the paper bags back to the supermarket.)

• write a letter to the Environmental Protection Agency (EPA) saying, "We're looking to you to do your best"?

• telephone some of the more activist women at the conference? ("Let's get together and see if we can't do something more meaningful. Since we're the key, we should demand homemakers on those boards. We could develop a tax-pollution campaign, with monies earmarked for ecology projects. How about collecting smashed cans and bags and delivering them to the EPA office with the press invited? We could tell them, 'We've collected them, now you find ways to recycle them.' *Something* to show that those buck-passers can't put the whole blame and responsibility on our shoulders.")

Action Coalitions Are Made, Not Born.

30.
JOINT ACTION

We all suffer from tunnel vision. Recognizing common interests in the abstract is just the beginning; working together despite very real conflicts and style differences is a "whole nother thing." Joint actions provide a readiness program to save us from the unhappy

YOU ARE THE KEY
TO THE ENVIRONMENT

HOW'S THAT ?

YOU CAN TAKE YOUR
CANS TO THE
RECYCLING CENTER

THEY SHUT
IT DOWN

THEN PUT 'EM IN
YOUR TRASH CAN

MAYBE YOU
ARE THE KEY TO
THE ENVIRONMENT

HOW'S THAT ?

YOU CAN QUIT
MAKING TRASH

experience of premature coalitions, while as the same time they extend effective action beyond a single organization. Here are just a few variations:

Parallel actions. Organizations that look at problems quite differently may still view other groups not as competitors but as potential allies. For example, the consumer movement may very well take off in the '70s. Since we are prime consumers, activist women should have a loud voice in forcing government agencies to regulate industries for people, rather than for the corporations they are supposed to control. Women's consumer groups can parallel women's rights, poverty, and ecology groups, and in the process move thousands of women from the passive to the active life. Both thoughtful consumers and social activists want to create a new kind of society, vague as its outlines may be. What is needed is a feminist approach to consumerism: an end to sex-role reinforcement through advertising; straight product information; realistic prices; money to buy the products industry creates (women and dependent children make up 85 percent of the poor); use of limited resources to provide for real needs; women's input where it counts . . . and more. That's how feminists might view consumer issues. Consumer organizations would state them differently, but there would be overlap, and no basic conflict of interest. They could work well on parallel actions. Each group could present its own testimony at a legislative hearing, for example.

Joint sponsorship. Groups with very little in common can often sponsor some project that does not entail much togetherness. Each group maintains a sense of separate identity. Food For All is a new OEO program directed by Graciela Olivarez of Phoenix, Arizona. Among its functions is to track down surplus food that never gets to the poor. Conceived in the spring of 1970 at the White House Conference of Food, Nutrition and Health, Food For All is sponsored by the League of Women Voters, National Council of Negro Women, American Friends Service Committee, National Federation of Settlements and Neighborhood Centers, Southwest Council of *La Raza,* and the National Urban Coalition. *The problem:* delivery of food to the hungry. *The sponsors:* a spectrum of "concerned-citizen" groups. The government pays the bill (a good formula when it works).

Joint suits. Groups working for the same ends in different fields may have a common grievance. By combining forces they strengthen their hand. In legal action, this is sometimes accomplished by filing a joint suit, as in a suit against the National Institutes of Health (NIH) filed by seven women's organizations. The suit charged that "women are virtually excluded from appointments as members of NIH public advisory groups" assigned to program policy. "We asked that the court forbid any further appointments of men to these public advisory groups until discriminatory policies against women are eliminated," said Sylvia Roberts of Baton Rouge, Louisiana, attorney. The suit was filed by the Association for Women in Science, the Association of Women in Psychology, Caucus of Women Biophysicists, Sociologists for Women in Society, Association for Women in Mathematics, National Organization for Women, and Women's Equity Action League.

Ad hoc-ing it. Joint action for a special purpose is a step toward coalition. Civil-rights issues, which usually entail legal battles, sometimes force diverse groups into working together. For example, in July 1970 the California Rural Legal Assistance filed a complaint against the State Public Utilities Commission, aimed at the fifteen hundred gas, electric, telephone, and water companies plus railroads, bus, and truck lines regulated by the Commission. Other organizations joining in the suit were the Western Regional NAACP, San Francisco NAACP, the Mexican-American Political Association, the Spanish-Speaking-Surnamed Political Association, the National Organization for Women, and the American GI Forum. The basis for the complaint was employment of minorities and women in low-paying positions and exclusion from upper-level management. The complaint demanded that the PUC order an affirmative-action policy of hiring and promoting blacks, Spanish-surnamed persons, and women. The action was announced at a joint press conference, attended by representatives of the organizations that had joined in the suit. Even such a minimal combined act as this is effective. Participating in a joint effort not only adds strength to the action itself, but provides the base for coalitions to come.

Join the party. Sometimes you are not invited into a collective action, but you feel you should be. Minority and student caucuses have changed the course of things by just barging in. (Sometimes to the good, sometimes like the bad fairy at Snow White's christening.)

In San Jose, California, a regional Democratic Party Conference discussed issues for the 1972 platform. Some members of NOW listened all morning to the male speakers. Over lunch they planned strategy. They divided up so that a feminist would present proposals in each afternoon workshop. Meanwhile a delegation went to conference planners, saying, "No input, no output." At each of the workshops (crime, national security, taxes, environment), proposals that incorporated women's views were adopted. Said one participant, "This probably won't make a dent on the National Democratic platform, but it did let the local yokels know that women's issues must be addressed."

Slates. When elections come (whether for political office or PTA), candidates will eye each other for combined vote-pulling strength. By pooling their constituencies they are more apt to be elected, as well as have more power once in office. For example, three candidates ran for the board of a consumers' co-op against more conservative incumbents. The slate consisted of a feminist who had been active in promoting an affirmative-action program for women and minorities, a black woman attorney, a white male supporter of the program. Each appealed to a different segment of voters, but all promoted the slate. By working together they could collect more campaign funds, maximize efforts, and promise a real change of policy if they won. Slate politics offers women a viable chance of breaking into electoral offices now generally closed to them.

Schools for community action. Humanitarian but timid organizations will sometimes participate in a joint body composed of women from several sponsoring groups. The new association, if comprised of the more activist members, can in its own name go further than its individual sponsors. Seattle women were quite successful with this form of alliance. Launched in 1965, the School for Community Action was sponsored by most of the "establishment" women's organizations: Archdiocesan Council of Catholic Women, Church Women United, Links, League of Women Voters, National Council of Jewish Women, National Council of Negro Women, and the YWCA. Its slogan—"toward an open society via woman power"—was activist. The primary function was education, organized through a yearly workshop. These conferences were successful because they attracted a cross section: white women and minorities, middle-class and poor, young and mature, radical and conservative, feminist and traditional. The input of all contributed to the flavor. The 1970 conference "New Perspectives for Women" stressed the common themes and problems that make women "more sensitive to each other." Areas of agreement included a proposal initiated by Councilwoman Jeannette Williams for a city Department of Women's Rights (since watered down to a Women's Commission by City Hall). Publication of a handbook for and by welfare recipients was a practical outcome. Never underestimate the power of a traditional women's group. Educate.

A common showcase. Organizations with differences of program and style are often willing to present themselves side by side. Each group does its own thing, allowing the observers to make their choices and draw their own conclusions. An excellent example occurred in Chicago in December 1971. At a press briefing for sympathetic media women, a whole gamut of Women's Liberation activities were presented. Representatives of nineteen groups gave short presentations and distributed press releases. The meeting was sponsored by *The Spokeswoman,* the Chicago Women's Liberation Union, NOW, and the YWCA's Loop Center.

Other versions of the showcase approach: an activities fair (often used in the ecology field); a forum, in which each group has equal time (*can* be deadly); literature tables (a standard for most jointly sponsored conferences).

The Coordinators and Facilitators

Every movement, for better or for worse, inspires the creation of myriad organizations. The women's movement will out-create the rest because it is so many-faceted, and because we all need experience in organizing. The variety will force us to create more new groups to coordinate those that already exist—at the very least, to provide communication so that we don't step on each other's toes. The grass-roots Women's Movement of Berkeley, which is antiorganization but proactivity, has found it necessary to have informal communications meetings about once a month to share with each other all the news. In addition, one group puts out a mimeographed newsletter with the sole purpose of keeping everyone informed of what's going on.

A promising new facilitator on the national level, the Women's Action Alliance, was at this writing just announced by Gloria Steinem. According to its statement, "Women will be working on local action projects which will help solve specific problems they face in their daily lives. Each project will create a model for action that can be duplicated by other women with similar needs." The Women's Action Alliance has opened a national office in New York City to provide the impetus and assistance for these grass roots efforts. The Alliance is already working with women in factories and universities to organize for childcare centers and maternity benefits.

The function of a facilitator is also performed by press. *The Spokeswoman,* an independent monthly newsletter of women's news, provides national coverage of women's activism, and performs an invaluable service to all feminists and their allies.

31. COALITIONS

We form coalitions for greater clout. We also form them for protection, because an individual organization is more vulnerable than a number of groups that stick together. Sometimes we form them to avoid flak from one's own membership, because a coalition is almost a separate entity, and anything too controversial can be laid at the door of this new body or its other members. Others are formed to give respectability to something not yet "respectable," or to create something new that can *move,* without cutting off roots. But most of all, coalitions are formed to put up a united front vis-à-vis the opposition.

Because the second wave of feminism is new, we haven't had

GROSS
CONGLOMERATE
PEOPLE'S
COALITION
CONSUMER
UNION
ACTION
COALITION
UNION OF
SECRETARIES
PEACE
UNION

... AND WE WILL DETERMINE OUR OWN LIVES.
PEOPLE'S
COALITION
ACTION
COALITION
PEACE
UNION

much experience with women's coalitions. Ever since the victory of suffrage, women's organizations (with some exceptions like peace groups) became essentially nonactivist, and individuals interested in causes pursued their concerns in organizations outside the "women's world." Without activism there is no great need for coalition. With the revival of feminism, coalitions are forming.

Significant Models

§ *Women United.* In 1924, when Congress first held hearings on the Equal Rights Amendment, sixteen women's organizations appeared to speak *against* it. The National Woman's Party was the sole supporter. Now, almost fifty years later, a large proportion of organized women endorse the amendment. Women United, formed in the spring of 1971, was a clearing-house coalition for the purpose of passing this constitutional change. Early feminists united their whole movement around the single issue of suffrage. To new feminists, a one-issue coalition provides a form for united action around this central demand, without hamstringing the Movement on other concerns. As stated by an activist in the coalition: "The absolutely only feminist issue we all agree on is the Amendment, and were conversation to stray from that subject for more than thirty seconds, the group might well disintegrate into a not-too-pleasant free-for-all."

§ *Network for Economic Rights.* NER was initiated by a labor union. "The group is a broad-based bipartisan coalition working together on state legislation applicable to men and women, and for enactment of legislative and executive orders of special import to females," according to Olga M. Madar, chairman (*sic*) pro tem. Participating groups take responsibility for task forces on specific issues: United Auto Workers concerns itself with the overtime question (contending it should be voluntary to the worker); YWCA works for abortion reform; WEAL concentrates on discrimination in universities; Michigan Welfare Rights works on welfare programs; American Federation of State, County and Municipal Employees (AFSCME) on civil-service discrimination and government-contract compliance; Communication Workers of

America (CWA) on maternity protection; NOW heads up child-care-center work; Hotel and Restaurant Workers are responsible for equal-pay and minimum-wage matters; the Women's Bar Association concentrates on legal and civil rights of all Michigan women. "A Legislative Alert" is the responsibility of all. These are "the big ten" issues, creating a united front for legislative action.

If a member group feels its policies are in conflict with those of NER, the group does not support action on that issue. As Olga Madar explained, "we realized that our differences on the Equal Rights Amendment were splitting us on other issues and we decided to get together. . . . We're showing the public and the lawmakers that we're not going to be split."

§ *Responsible Corporate Action.* Women's rights groups are beginning to work effectively in coalition with other excluded sectors.

"Our coalition will seek to bring about a change in this corporate apartheid," declared Leonard H. Carter, regional director of the NAACP. The coalition of thirteen black, Spanish-speaking, and women's organizations aims at making the major California firms designate 25 percent of their directors' positions to women and members of minority groups. "We're going to organize women stockholders to speak on women's issues in corporations," said Aileen Hernandez, then president of the National Organization for Women. How does such a coalition work? Primarily through press conferences, printed reports, and speaking out at stockholders' meetings. Its purpose is to generate the public pressure set by Ralph Nader which resulted in appointment of the first black director by General Motors. Speaking out together, these minority and women's groups expose the real minority that holds current corporate leadership, white males over forty. A united front of excluded sectors puts corporations on the defensive, and will eventually force concessions. It also reinforces pressures for affirmative action programs.

General coalition principles are a program broad enough to appeal to diverse interests, specific enough to be clearly understood by member organizations, shared responsibility and leadership

WHAT CAN I DO
I'M ONLY ONE WOMAN
WHAT CAN WE DO
WE'RE ONLY A FEW WOMEN
WOMEN UNITE
EQUAL RIGHTS NOW
My fellow citizens Women belong
IN PUBLIC OFFICE

among participating groups, and mutual self-interest (I'll help you if you'll help me). A solid coalition groundwork spells power.

Coalition Politics

"It's going to take a combination—women, blacks, Chicanos, Indians—all in a salad bowl, not a melting pot," said Shirley Chisholm, campaigning for presidency of the United States. "If we're mature enough to form this coalition, we could deal a death blow to the forces that have controlled this country. . . . Just because government has been an exclusive domain of rich, white males, does not mean it always need be. . . . Women have the potential to draw together that kind of coalition."

Politicians have to think coalition. Juggling the interests of their various constituencies is the political staff of life, at least before elections. (Afterward, with the rare exceptions of those who are "unbossed and unbought," the lobbyists take over.) But the concept of women as a group, not as individuals, and as a separate constituency worth talking to seriously, is a by-product of the revival of feminism.

Political coalitions rarely take organizational form. They usually consist of a combination of bedfellows (or is it "bed persons"?) who support a candidate, but may not be on speaking terms with each other. Nevertheless, they do provide a sense of "our side." More important for us is the emergence of an informal coalition—or a caucus—of women. The new constituency is organizing.

National Women's Political Caucus

It is dangerous to predict the adult at the moment of christening, but if ever there were an embodiment of an idea whose time has come, it's the Caucus. Over three hundred women of varied interests attended the organizing conference in July 1971. Press and politicians took careful note. As many women vote as men, but until now that hasn't signified much. The Caucus aims to change that. Among its most cogent goals:

—To rally national support for women candidates who declare themselves ready to fight, not only for the needs of women, but for all underrepresented groups.

—To hold caucuses on a state and local level; to register new women voters and encourage women to vote for women's priorities.

—To see that each state delegation of the two national political conventions in 1972 was no less than 50 percent women.

—To form coalitions with other oppressed groups and all groups that share similar humane goals: fighting sexism, racism, violence, and poverty.

"Women," said feminist writer Gloria Steinem, "must create a new kind of 'human politics': Our aim would be to humanize society by bringing the values of women's culture into it, not simply to put individual women into men's places."

Well, that's the goal, and it's a good one. Already the Caucus's input was reflected in the Democratic Party's National Reform Commission proposals for the party convention, according to which women should comprise half the delegates. If carried through, that would be a great leap forward. That doesn't take care of other problems: the lethargy and the opportunism, and discovering that being female doesn't immunize against corruption. But Summer '72 women were a recognized constituency for the first time. No longer will sex appeal of a candidate be the only criterion for the women's vote, for we are a legitimate part of coalition politics. (As one woman in New York said of Mayor John Lindsay when he was a candidate for the Democratic nomination for president, "I wouldn't vote for him, but I would like to spend the weekend with him.") Our issues will have to be listened to, not because we are "right," but because organized womanhood, or even a significant sector, can deliver and withhold votes.

Are we really ready for coalition?

Problems of Coalition

It's so much easier to see the common ground than to occupy it together. The first step is to recognize some of the difficulties that keep us divided.

The very real contradictions

There are classes and races in this society as well as sexes. Because the conditions we live under vary so much, one woman's liberation can be another woman's chains. If middle-income white women feel liberated and go out and work, who will look after the children? "We will, of course," answer some black women. "All those fine management jobs for white women will just make us worse off by comparison." How are such contradictions to be faced? In this case good childcare facilities are one part of the answer. But more generally, we will learn that the most solid progress for all comes through advancement of those on the bottom of the heap.

On the other hand, one woman's bondage can be another's liberation. A fine film of the '50s, *Salt of the Earth,* shows Mexican-American women daring to break their homebound culture to form a women's auxiliary to a labor union on strike. In that context, serving coffee to the men on the picket lines was a liberating victory. Understanding context is essential for coalitions.

Another example of the same principle: Paraprofessionalism in the medical, teaching, and legal fields is usually seen as a rung in a ladder upward for less-educated women, but when female college graduates fill paraprofessional positions at pay about half what a man would make, with increased status but low salary, you have "new shanties on the old plantations." In other words, there are basic differences in this society. If sisterhood has real meaning, we will be sensitive to those differences and make sure that some sisters don't "liberate" themselves on the backs of others. That's not real liberation anyway.

One-up-womanship

Unfortunately, organizations compete with each other. Often it seems their favorite activity. Even with lots of good will, cooperation is hard to achieve, harder than within a single organization. (If we're not as competitive as men's groups, it's partly that we've had less to scrap over.) There seems to be a universal urge (culturally conditioned, perhaps) to be more than—stronger than—louder than—smarter than. All of which, hopefully, will fade. In general, when any one organization is one-up, others feel one-down.

When dogs bark . . .

The thief throws a bone. A number of groups unite for a good childcare program. At last, a minimal program is funded, but the unity dissolves in the scramble for which group will be the sponsoring organization. Opposition invariably tries to divide a coalition, one way or another. A bone is an effective way.

Too many issues

The right to differ on everything else than the purpose(s) for which the coalition was formed should be held inviolable. Too often an insensitive member insists on pushing the area of agreement too far. Out of the controversy, the coalition breaks up.

Trashing, redbaiting, and red blackmail

Attacking people (not ideas) is trashing. Redbaiting is attacking a person or group for radical leanings or affiliation, not for performance within a coalition. Red blackmail is the opposite: countering any differences of policy with accusations of redbaiting. A lot of counterproductive in-fighting of these types goes on in the name of principle, when tact and diplomacy are sorely needed. A coalition is a delicate plant. Nurture it.

Sex and gender

As we all know, it is quite possible to be of the female gender while denying all identification with other women. A feminist, on the other hand, may be of either gender, but is sympathetic to what the Women's Movement is all about. In working in any coalition, decide whether you are talking about sex or gender. It has little value to ensure female representation if the females don't identify themselves as such. For example, are you asking for a feminist on the board (male or female)? Or a woman (pro-woman or not)? Or a woman who is also a feminist?

Sex and race

It happened in the first wave of feminism, and it's happening again. The rights of blacks and white women *appear* to be in conflict. When the "Negro's hour" came in 1865, feminists tried desperately to link suffrage for women and blacks. When they failed, they sometimes used white-supremacy arguments to further their own cause—unsuccessfully.

The growth of Women's Liberation, stimulated by the civil-rights movement of the early 1960s, imitated the black protest movement in rhetoric and style. Women used blacks to describe themselves (women as niggers); to protest any point (you wouldn't dare treat a black person like that!); as proof of oppression (the average black male earns more than the average white female—a racist argument, sometimes prefaced with "even . . ."). This is understandably galling to black leaders who feel the impetus of the hard-fought civil-rights battle diverted by white females who want to capitalize on their efforts. The real friction comes in competition for jobs in affirmative action programs. Yet even here the conflict of interest is more apparent than real. Chairman Brown of the Equal Employment Opportunities Commission (a black man) has pointed out repeatedly that discrimination is discrimination. If you investigate for sex, you discover race bias, and vice versa. Added pressure to overcome the "pale-male" monopoly will speed the time when each individual is judged on merit. Soon we will all be out of a job if we don't create a human-need–oriented economy.

The Women's Movement is unduly sensitive to the fact that it is composed largely of white women (usually designated as middle-class, although a large percentage of us recognize we are Have-nots). There is an unnecessary sense of guilt for organizing in our own interests. We cite statistics as though there were a contest for most oppressed. We don't listen when third-world women patiently explain why they must work within their own groups. Most important, we don't seek out the common ground. By and large the solid ground is issues.

Lifestyle, class, race, culture—all create their own rhetorics. Psychic oppression is different from hungry oppression, and it is hard to relate to the slogans of a different culture, but a childcare center is a childcare center. Some of our priorities will differ, some will coincide. As in all coalition work, maximize the common interests and respect the differences. This time around, it's every body's hour, or nobody's.

One Dozen Coalition-Builders

(1) *Establish yourself first.* Go in with some trading stamps of your own. An organization with a proven constituency is listened to quite differently from one with a good cause but no followers. If you don't have numbers, then be sure to have some other kind of organizational currency (like money, ideas, information, guts).

(2) *Set positive ground rules early.* Anticipating differences in style, work out the *modus operandi* before problems arise. ("I understand you handle this . . . We do it differently. How shall our coalition do it?")

(3) *Build linkages within coalition memberships.* No delegate can really speak for all the members. If we have more than one pipeline into an organization, we have better insight of how fast or how slow the coalition should go. ("Your annual meeting? Yes, I'll have a ticket. I'd like to meet some of your members and find out more what you do.") The delegate will probably introduce you to the others.

(4) *I'll scratch your back.* Suppose two women's groups—an ecology-oriented association and a Native-American organization—have decided to work for the defeat of a certain land-development bill in the state legislature. Each approaches the matter from a different angle. The Native-Americans have the biggest personal stake: the legislation will affect their fishing rights. The ecology group is especially concerned with water pollution. The women have a general interest in environmental matters and a special desire to become more politically effective. The coalition concentrates on this particular piece of legislation (testifying, speaking, sending out press releases, and promoting letters within the member organizations). At the same time, they agree to publicize within their groups other bills that any of their members have taken stands on, and which don't conflict with their own policies. With luck and hard work, the coalition will continue if and when the bill is defeated.

(5) *Hot Line.* Either as part of the coalition, or as a step in building it, an action network increases clout. Take the situation just described. Whenever an issue is at a point and a specific action is needed, a participant notifies the coalition and word is spread quickly, usually by telephone. If each organization within the coalition has a telephone tree of some sort, a real response can be generated fast. An action network or hot line is especially good to put pressure on legislators, or to fill a hall at a hearing. It takes some effort to organize, but it is not only productive, it involves people. Women do well communicating by phone, so we should use this to our advantage.

(6) *The springboard principle.* Coalitions are easiest to form on a temporary, ad hoc basis, because that is less threatening to existing groups, and demands less commitment of time and personnel. A joint conference is a good starting point. In making the event a success, a new working collective grows. Often the conference can be a springboard for continued cooperation between the sponsors, or even give birth to an ongoing coalition.

(7) *Locate the responsive sub-body.* If a large organization is not prepared to move along with us, perhaps some part of it will. In most organizations there are subgroups, committees, or task forces that are more activist-minded. If an invitation to participate in some project seems to fall on deaf ears, maybe there

are other more willing ones. Ask for the social-concerns committee of a church, public-affairs committee of a women's organization, or the action chairperson.

(8) *Working for the future.* Where groups cannot unite in one coalition because their immediate interests conflict (as in sex and race), parallel coalitions may cooperate. Organizers from Alinsky's Areas Foundation Training Institute tried a unique approach in Gary, Indiana. The Calumet Community Congress, made up of primarily white churches, women's organizations, labor unions, suburban-betterment groups, and so forth, held a congress and agreed to a ten-point action program to combat pollution and political corruption, focusing pressure on the giant steel mills that have made Gary one of the dirtiest communities in America. Meanwhile, a parallel coalition of black organizations was under way. "We are talking about a new model where people deal with each other from a position of strength and power," said Obadiah Simms, a black organizer. Granting the dangers of separate organization, the approach may be fruitful, especially for cooperation on civil-rights issues.

(9) *Expand the circle.* One of the best things about coalition action is that it enlarges the circle of contacts. If a number of organizations band together, we can be quite sure that we will have some friends on the opposition home ground: "Does anyone have any members that work for that company?" "Any possibility we could get the inside facts?" Or resources: "How could we get the use of a church?" "We'll need to move equipment. Does anyone have a member with access to a truck?" All these things have double value: they get the job done, and they involve more people.

(10) *Inside-outside alliances.* Those inside contacts can become important allies. Perhaps there is an incipient women's caucus brewing in a government department. For job-security reasons, the women may not be able to join our coalition, but informally may be delighted to work with us—a fruitful two-way relationship. An asset of great potential to the Women's Movement is its ubiquitousness. You never can tell whose secretary is a not-so-latent feminist!

(11) *The spectrum approach.* A coalition should be as broad a spectrum as possible, and still be able to work together. Too disparate in style or politics, and the coalition breaks up; too simi-

lar, and we haven't accomplished much by coalescing. It depends in part on readiness to accept differences, prior experience in working together, and a lot of personalities.

(12) *Moving down the middle.* Since coalition action is essentially compromise, if we want our view to carry the day, we had better have voices to either side of ours. A more militant view will make us sound reasonable; a timid position makes us sound bold.

32.
THE CONFERENCE

Somewhere down the line most organizations and coalitions decide to hold a conference. For women, it's a very acceptable form: a break in the routine, nonthreatening, a chance to meet old friends and new, and something to fill the gnawing inside for "self-improvement." For the leaders, at least, there's a sense of accomplishment. Most women's conferences perform these functions quite well, but they seldom challenge the power structure. And when it's all over, the good energy peters out.

In planning a conference, the most important single factor is *knowing what you want,* says a professional conference organizer. Then the goals must be translated into a call (or announcement) that should be intriguing but not intimidating to the women we want to come.

The first planning phase is crucial. Conferences have a way of starting out with one function and shifting to another. The original intent gets sidetracked, so planners should keep stating and restating the purpose.

Once that's cleared up, decide on time and place, which are not trivial questions by any means. Size up the competition: holidays, sports schedules if relevant, and the work schedules and family patterns of those you want most to attend.

A Conference Budget

"First and foremost," says our pro, "establish your conference budget." This largely revolves around the crystal-ball gazing task of forecasting the hidden costs:

EXPENSES	INCOME
Promotion: paper, printing, postage, publicity	*Registrations:* (allow for no-pays—the poor, unemployed, and students)
Arrangements: rent, phone, mimeo	*Donations:* (from sponsoring groups or individuals)
Registration: kits, badges	*Sponsorships or scholarships*
Speakers: fees, expenses	*Donations in kind* (e.g., phone, clerical, or mailing)
Hidden and forgotten costs: (plan for them or be sorry)	*Fund raising event or appeal:* (as part of conference)
Follow up costs: reports, thank-yous, action	*Sale of materials:*

In deciding budget questions, always refer back to purpose. With speakers, if you are paying only expenses, put it in writing. "Even if the person in question is your own mother," says the pro.

Some conferences have a paying sponsor—a university, foundation, or affluent group that underwrites a substantial share of the costs. WARNING: They can limit your action.

A good mix of people, more important than numbers, can make a conference click. Diversity is the key. Don't give up easily on the hard-to-get (like welfare mothers). Take extra time and effort, and offer a "carrot" (hard-pressed poor women will not spend precious time talking about problems unless they can see some concrete advantage to their own group).

Who speaks is the next crucial question. A weak keynoter won't kill a conference, but a really effective one will get it off to a head start. Cost (expenses and/or honorarium), drawing appeal, status all must be considered, but give major weight to "karma," and ability to express what it is that you want to accomplish. Next in line come workshop leaders, who should be representative of the groups involved, but also fair and forceful. Choose persons who will neither dominate nor allow discussion to wander.

Conference follow-up is the most neglected ingredient. See the conference as a beginning, not an end. But you're tired. Other responsibilities have been piling up ("As soon as this conference is over . . ."). So women usually settle for thank-you notes, and sometimes a written report to the participants, two months later. Consider how wasteful this is.

Go back to the purpose: Why was it called in the first place? Someone has to grab hold of that moment, pull tired people together in spite of themselves, draw in fresh forces turned on by the event, call another meeting if necessary, and plan to carry out the mandate of the conference. Was it to organize a coalition? Move right into it. To take an issue to the press and public? Call a press conference with the best newsmaking people and ideas.

There are times when a collective works well (as in planning a conference); there are also times when one super-dedicated person can execute what a group desires. At least she can set the example. If, from the beginning, the conference is seen as the impetus for the next step, it will be much easier to ride with the momentum.

Soon, before the glow is dimmed, evaluate the whole thing. (Where did we start from, where did we go, and where are we going now?) What were the purposes, again, and how well were they achieved? What are the specific do's and don'ts for the next time around? What special "strokes" should be given—to individuals and to the group as a whole? And of course, where do we go from here?

A Conference Checklist

—Allow plenty of time to recover from calamities. Nail things down early (purpose, date, place, key speakers). Work like the devil in the beginning.

—The call should be ready early enough so that sponsoring organizations can include it in their regular mailings. Announcements are generally mailed at least one month in advance.

—How about physical arrangements? Enough room for workshops, general sessions, parking, displays, registration area? Child-care is a must for women's conferences.

—Preregistration, if any. Foresee bottlenecks at the door. Name tags or badges. Voting cards if needed.

—Kits. Too much is self-defeating. Try to boil down to the agenda and the most relevant tools to accomplish the purpose.

—Food. Whether it's a brown bag or a hotel-catered affair, plan it, for people will eat. Consider price. Coffee and tea soothe jangled nerves.

—Display and sales. Opportunity to promote a pet project will make participating organizations more cooperative. So, if possible, allow space for tables. Ensure a full spectrum to reflect the coalition.

—If many resolutions are anticipated, a resolution committee is desirable. Groups participating will need some ground rules. For formal conferences, a rules committee is necessary, and a parliamentarian. There should be duplicating facilities at the conference itself.

—Press planning includes prepublicity, getting media people there, interviews, and press conference if possible. Locate sympathetic newswomen who might attend. Don't forget newsletters and specialized press of sponsoring organizations. Plan in visual items for news photos and TV.

—All talk can be dull. Music and skits will change the pace, and also heighten emotional involvement.

—Fine action ideas may emerge spontaneously, but don't count on it. Plan one or more to unify the gathering.

—Consider whether follow-up should take organizational form. If so, plan for it in advance.

—Keep the conference relatively on schedule. Pace it. Don't let it get bogged down or diverted. Keep the purposes before the body.

—Develop a sense of common ground (areas of agreement), the discovery of which is in itself an accomplishment. Without minimizing the differences, emphasize the collective.

—Workshop accomplishment should be tangible: a report to the main body, resolutions, material to be incorporated into a conference report, a task force to follow up after the conference. Consider skills or project workshops as well as issues.

—People never divide themselves up evenly for workshops. "Give any hundred people their head and fifty of them will stampede for the same seminar room, where they will swelter in a room equipped for twenty, while somewhere else five people and a discouraged leader will rattle around in lonely splendor, wondering where all the action is," says our professional. Preregistration for workshops sometimes helps. Expect to do some improvising.

—In choosing leadership (chairpersons, resources, reporters), avoid both the narrow specialist and the rambling lecturer. If possible, brief beforehand, so everyone is on the same wavelength. At least provide in writing the purpose, what the leader's role is, and detailed instructions. They will thank you for it.

—Now relax and enjoy. A conference is a social gathering, and the hostesses must not be uptight.

I HAVE FULLY GRASPED THE SITUATION!
BUT THE SITUATION *HAS CHANGED AGAIN!*

Creating the Phoenix while Rome Burns

POLITICS HAS FAILED ME

REVOLUTION HAS FAILED ME

RELIGION HAS FAILED ME

DROPPING OUT HAS FAILED ME

MAYBE FAILURE HAS FAILED ME

33.
WHY DO WE KEEP TRYING TO BUILD WHILE THE FLAMES ROAR?

Because if there is to be a New Society, everybody has to learn carpentry. Consider all this activism as an apprenticeship for the big job ahead, as a people's urban renewal. By the time we have practiced regular push-ups, organized ourselves, banded together and initiated some group actions, and experienced coalition activity, we will all have learned a few things. We will have discovered that institutional change does not just happen. We will have traveled down some dead ends, and discovered that these are part of the trip. We will have a much better idea of who are the builders and who are the spoilers. And, I suspect, we will begin to envision what the future could be.

The Phoenix Redefined

"You can't hold back progress," we're told when a new high-rise is proposed or a conglomerate is formed. Progress *has* been held back in the social sphere, however, to the point that long-outmoded institutions are seriously out of kilter with the way goods and services are produced. In the long run you can't hold back progress in development of social systems and human institutions any more than you can technological ones. Changes are coming whether we like it or not, for when an ecological system is on a collision course with an economic system, something has to give. When delivery of

bulbul-72

goods and services are out of line with expectations, tensions increase until something pops.

If changes are coming, we had better be in there deciding which changes, how fast, and in what direction. Human needs is our field of expertise, so let's say it out loud: They need us.

It won't be easy to avoid the old service trap. The suffragists of the latter nineteenth century argued that the gentler nature of women would make war obsolete if only women had the vote. They believed their own pedestal role. In fact, it will take a tough, self-interested, committed Women's Movement, and countless individuals and knots of women everywhere working in the same general direction toward a more humane society. And along the way they will need to join forces with other powerless peoples. Inevitably, a tremendous amount of learning will take place. Sisterhood (and, yes, brotherhood) will have to become more than an abstraction. Active intervention in the affairs of state can be the process by which new forces will evolve. The phoenix is us.

The Major Pitfalls

Even after we get our heads together, and we think we know (in general) what needs to be done, working for social change is like proceeding down a path beset with pitfalls. To get anywhere at all, we must learn to recognize some of them:

Co-option

Nothing much will be changed merely by adding a woman or two to a formerly all-male body. Such tokenism may be expected as women become more vocal. Co-option is the process whereby a vocal critic of an institution is invited in and, once inside, adopts the same priorities and limitations that brought on the criticism in the first place. One test for co-option: Could I lose the job (or position of status) without being shattered? It is possible to work on the inside without being co-opted, but you have to be an independent agent.

Secondly, working inside the system requires continual compromise. Working anywhere does, but if you are on the outside it is easier to stay pure. On the inside you are walking a tightrope between principles and pressures. A second test for co-option: On what principles would I *not* compromise?

ALL THOSE IN FAVOR OF THE QUICKIE-KILL BOMB PROJECT

Band-Aids

Learn to distinguish between what can be done (easily) and what should be done. Lean toward the latter. For example, Women in Community Service (WICS) have worked diligently to help disadvantaged young women break out of the cycle of poverty and deprivation. Many of these teen-agers are children of parents from rural communities. At the same time all of us, including WICS, pay taxes to subsidize corporate farmers who drive the rural poor to the cities. As women we learn of their suffering and want to help. So we reach out our hands to soothe a brow, or perhaps aid an individual out of compassion for her plight. What could we do instead? We could cry out; we could expose; we could demand that farming not be used as a tax shelter by rich individuals and corporations, and raise the question of land reform. But what about those that are already victims of the system? Until we stop the flow, there will be more and more such victims for us to *serve.* What we can do for them is to support their struggles for jobs and adequate income. It's harder to prescribe surgery than to apply Band-Aids, but cancer spreads and finally destroys the body.

The sidetrack

Anyone who has been part of a delegation to Authority has experienced polite pressure to deflect the confrontation into a new and harmless path. ("It's just wonderful you ladies are so concerned. But you're going about it the wrong way. What you really ought to be doing is . . .") As women become a real threat to the status quo, efforts will be increased to sidetrack them. At a recent business-oriented conference on consumerism, an official stated:

> I don't think it is an exaggeration to say that many frustrated housewives, trapped into the drudgery of mundane household chores, unable to sustantially change their lot, are the shock troops of today's conservation, ecology, and consumerism movements.

These fields could easily serve to deflect the new feminism in the same way as the settlement-house movement provided an outlet for the discontent of our grandmothers. This time we must not let it happen. Conservation, ecology, and consumerism are just as valid human concerns as any other when taken seriously. But settlement houses did not get at the causes of poverty, and women's role changed very little. This time we must go all the way to the roots of the issue—to basic shifts of power.

Counterculture

The earth mother in a hippie commune may escape a plastic culture only to learn that our foremothers' life was not so rewarding. The Carrie Chapman Catts and the Susan B. Anthonys fought back precisely against that role. Antimaterialism is to the good, also the complete rejection of militarism. And certainly the efforts to create alternative institutions ("food conspiracies," free clinics, communal lifestyles) challenge outmoded assumptions taken for granted too long. But the pitfall is to see such innovations as the answer.

Middle-class versions of utopian communities may be more comfortable than the subsistence style of the young. But they add more to the problem than to the solution, for they perpetuate the myth that freedom (or liberation or peace or an ecologically sound society) is a matter of personal choice. Unfortunately, we are all tied to one another.

All or nothing

In the back of any activist's mind is the realistic fear that any reform that ameliorates a bad scene without coping with the underlying problem only blunts the discontent and postpones eventual solution. But not all reforms are Band-Aids. In the same manner that we can learn to distinguish between service-oriented and change-oriented volunteerism, we can distinguish between reforms that preserve the status quo (be it woman's role, racial inequality, or the hegemony of the military-industrial complex) and those that shift the power into new and popular hands. For example, any change that strengthens the feminist voice in decision-making bodies is more than a Band-Aid. It puts an ally on the inside. If we wait for the revolution, it will never come.

Somehow the nuts and the berries don't make it easier to breathe.

Elitism

Any self-styled vanguard runs the risk of considering itself an elite appointed to guide the less enlightened out of darkness. In this era, everybody has something to offer and everyone's input is needed. More serious are divisive tactics that put down efforts to achieve results short of total victory. (As if there is such a thing as total victory!)

Leave it to the next generation

They may sound like they have all the answers, but don't believe it. "Consciousness III" is a comforting thought to tired ac-

tivists who would like to relax and let the more vigorous young pick up the torch. Unfortunately, no one segment can turn things around (not even women). Up! Rest period's over. You never sat down? Good! The next generation will thank you. (Think of the honor the long-maligned "premature feminists" are receiving today.)

ELITISM

Let the kids make the revolution.

34.
WHERE WILL IT ALL LEAD?

Every layer peeled off the onion reveals another one. And the deeper you dig, the more your eyes water. (No wonder we prefer to buy chopped onions in plastic bags.)

If we say, "What's the use? It's senseless—might as well live a little," disasters will eventually catch up with us or our children.

If we say, "Seize the power!", we soon find we can't.

If we wait for the revolution, any activity we have going dies out.

The only other alternatives are to take *some* of the power, block the spoilers, define and fight for human needs, and lay the foundation for a better world to come.

The right questions are better than the wrong answers

So you don't know how the complex, bureaucrat-ridden problem can be solved, but you do know that the present situation hurts. They will tell you to go away if you can't come up with The Answer. Don't. Stay on the firm ground of human need, and keep asking:

When is enough? (Megatons, concrete, medical prices, smog, water pollution, bombs . . .)

What will the children inherit? (Will there be anything left?)

Who speaks for the losers? (And who listens?)

Is greed the only force that can keep an economy going?

Why? (The best question. The emperor has no clothes, but nobody says so.)

The continued probing questions will have an affect, not the least of which is that sooner or later we will come up with the right answers ourselves.

What about the side effects?

That is what worries so many. Taking a giant step always involves a risk, to both the individuals concerned and the social fabric. Responsibility for change is frightening, for "the man's" world is hostile. We would endure incredible situations rather than risk the unknown. "Revolution? How revolting!"

Now turn away from the social scene and look at the less familiar (for us) technological kingdom, usually called Progress. Here a quite different mood prevails. Every new development is hailed as a breakthrough and great boon to mankind (*sic*). Never mind the side effects. Never mind the long-range consequences. Revolution in technology is not only continuous, but is lavishly rewarded.

Women's interests and training are overwhelmingly concerned with those basic human needs of food, clothing and well-being. Men's interests and training generally gravitate to that technological world with all its associated structures. Anyone with eyes in his or her head can see that the two spheres are out of balance.

For the past hundred years, at an increasing rate, technology has created rapid change. By contrast, social institutions have altered much more slowly. Like those earth masses on two sides of a fault line, tensions have increased to a dangerous level. Unless there are some friendly quakes to relieve the situation, disaster is coming. How you define a friendly quake depends on how desperate you feel the situation is, and how big a shake you think is needed. If you believe that we are bottoming out, at least in regard to the quality of our lives and our chances for survival, you will risk more. But isn't it better to be part of the shaking than the shaken?

After the quake, the two spheres will be in better alignment, with men and women more equally balanced on both sides. Only then can technology really be put to service for human needs.

Price tags for social change

The trouble is, everybody wants a change, but nobody wants to pay for it. We would like to have fewer cars on the road but not give up our own; less waste of natural resources, but a department store filled with gadgets; equal rights, but permission to fall back on feminine helplessness if necessary. We're also very generous with human rights for others so long as it doesn't affect our own neighborhoods.

There is one ray of hope for that dilemma. Giving up something is much easier when everyone has to give it up together. When you can't have something that your neighbor has, that's tough, but when you both have to do without, you shrug your shoulders and make do. Those who can remember the Depression look back with some nostalgia at their shared deprivations. Meat stamps during World War II were a nuisance, but they did equalize matters somewhat, and encouraged some very creative recipes. When an emergency occurs, as in the great New York blackout, humanity flowers and people are more resourceful. All of which is just to point out that "human nature" does change—when it has to.

The fun is in the going

The truth is that life has more zest if we participate actively in it, despite risks, setbacks, wasted effort, and even deprivation. Existentialists and doctors say so. Social-minded religionists believe it too. Newly activated women know so. When they give themselves permission to *go,* they feel an exhilaration that astounds them, accompanied by anger for prior passivity. There is almost a religious fervor in the new feminism.

Older women have the most to gain from coming out of their protected shells, because they have the least to lose, so far as self-esteem is concerned. In our society, aging is a losing battle, and most of the supposed compensations turn to gall. Women over forty whose children are turning outward feel that life has passed them by; they need activism as much as they are needed by an ailing society. For a new lease on life, effective social involvement is far better than a psychiatrist, and much cheaper. "Volunteer for something" fits the old concept of womanhood. "Help turn the world around" is more appropriate today.

35. FREEDOM AND RESPONSIBILITY: A FEMINIST VIEW

What is a feminist? Wilma Scott Heide, President of NOW, defines it:

> A person who believes women (even as men) are primarily people; that human rights are indivisible by any category of sex, race, class, or other designation irrelevant to our common humanness. Furthermore, a feminist is committed to creating the equality (not sameness) of the sexes legally, socially, educationally, psychologically, politically, religiously, economically, in and out of the home.

Feminism is the Women's Rights and Liberation movements with all their variations of purpose and style. But more fundamentally, it is a new concept of the female self. You don't have to be a member of anything to be a feminist; you do have to think like one.

You certainly don't have to make a choice between feminism and humanism, because the two are ultimately synonymous. Nor do you have to desert the cause of peace to work for women's rights, but a feminist will work for peace with her sisters in mind. You don't have to forget about civil rights—in fact, you can't, because rights are indivisible. But when you work for civil rights for minorities, you won't negate your own. If saving the environment is where you want to put your energy, you will seek out women's special stake and contribution.

In trying to get back to ourselves, feminists rightly concentrated on women's immediate needs, and the psychological affects of assigning women to a limited and supportive role. It was generally stated, "Stop working for other causes when we ourselves are in chains." Now we have a woman's consciousness, a movement of some breadth and variation, and greater recognition that women can and must participate in all aspects of life. Some will do better in one field, some in another. Issues affecting women are so numerous and so interrelated that anyone can choose her own priorities. Seeing woman's work as encompassing the globe need not distract the Woman's Movement. Rather, such a vision provides the cohesion that is central to sisterhood.

A feminist is an active, participating member of society. She is liberated in the sense that she feels free of the inhibiting effects of sex-assigned roles. "Choices" is a favorite word in the Women's Movement, and feminists work for more of them. A woman should have the right to work (at equal pay with equal opportunity) if she wants to, and she should have the right to choose not to. When she's selecting a field, she should not be limited to traditionally female employment. Marriage should be an option, not an assumed career that carries penalties if she doesn't "make it." If she wants children, fine; if not, that's her right (including the right to terminate an unwanted pregnancy).

These are choices, the providing of which is at the core of the women's struggle. But . . . *more choices* → *more decisions* →

more responsibility for decisions made. Unfortunately, we can't have the one without the other. So freedom and responsibility are paired for women, as they are for everyone else in society. More choices is a heavier load in some ways, but more rewarding in others. Some women will rejoice; others will tremble.

For men, especially for those who need to feel superior to somebody, there may be some loss of ego. But I believe they will accept more than we think they will (if they have to). For a large number of men there will be short-term losses and long-term gains. The transition will be rough.

The new feminism goes much deeper than its predecessor, because the conditions that created it are far more desperate. We are not talking about a "bigger slice of the pie," but a whole new recipe. No more indigestible crust or chemical ingredients that simulate natural flavors. We'll bake a pie fit to set before the human race, or we'll all eat crow.

bulbul

Notes and Sources

Part I

The advice on *How To Put Your Husband Through College* was given by Barbara Ream Debrodt (New York: Harper & Row, 1970). Lucy Graves Mayo provided the office hints in *You Can Be an Executive Secretary* (London: Collier Macmillan Ltd., 1965). Anne David's A Guide to Volunteer Services (New York: Cornerstone Library, 1970) gave advice in that area.

There has not been a great deal published as yet on consciousness-raising small groups for Women's Liberation. The section quoted is from *Free Space* by Pamela Allen (New York: Times Change Press, 1970). The comments were gleaned from a Berkeley conference in 1971, "Small Groups and Beyond."

One of the most influential feminist books in the last decade was Betty Friedan's *The Feminine Mystique* (New York: W. W. Norton, 1963), to which I owe a great debt of gratitude, as do all feminists.

The letters in *Write On* are excerpted from my pamphlet of that title prepared for NOW (1957 E. 73rd St., Chicago, Ill. 60649), and suggested by letters to the editor from various papers.

In the anthology *Woman in Sexist Society*, edited by Vivian Gornick and Barbara K. Moran (New York: Basic Books, 1971), are two valuable articles pertaining to volunteerism. Doris Gold's "Women and Voluntarism" was one of the first feminist critiques of volunteer activity as an extension of women's traditional role. Margaret Adams explores "The Compassion Trap" that turns women's strengths back against them.

"Volunteer Beware" is a pamphlet available from Berkeley NOW (P.O. Box 7024, Berkeley, Ca. 94707). The Council on Economic Priorities has offices in New York City, Washington, D.C., and San Francisco (West Coast address: P.O. Box 2210, San Francisco, Ca. 94129).

The analogy of career ladders for women to those of the poor came from reading Arthur Pearl and Frank Riessman, *New Careers for the Poor* (New York: The Free Press, 1965).

Dorothy Samuel (2809 Southern Ave., Baltimore, Md. 21214)

sent out the letter "Let's Call a Halt" to women's organizations all over the country. As a result, NOW set up a Task Force on Women and Volunteerism, to study this issue.

Part II

"Banding Together"

Consumer Action Now, Inc. (815 Park Ave., New York, N.Y. 10001) issues a monthly magazine, *CAN*. For a list of other consumer groups, send 25¢ and a self-addressed, stamped business-size envelope to *McCall's* magazine (Consumer List, Rm. 766A, 230 Park Ave., New York, N.Y. 10017).

Join Hands (P.O. Box 49944, Los Angeles, Ca. 90049) has numerous pamphlets besides the pledge. Members of the Kitsap County, Washington, chapter of NOW were so pleased with their organizational success that they have written a useful booklet, "Starting a Chapter of NOW; a Practical Handbook for Women in Small Cities, Towns and Rural Areas" (write to Nancy Filler, Rt. 6, Box 6854, Bainbridge Island, Wash. 98110).

The Berkeley Women's Health Collective, which in April 1972 had just received a small grant from the Berkeley City Council, is located at Trinity United Methodist Church, 2320 Dana St., Berkeley, California.

The women's caucus of the Modern Language Association is described in the MLA Newsletter, Vol. 3, No. 1, Feb., 1971 (62 Fifth Ave., New York, N.Y. 10011). The Women's Equity Action League (WEAL, c/o Women's City Club of Cleveland, Bulkley Bldg., Cleveland, Ohio 44115) also publishes a fine monthly legislative summary, *WEAL Washington Report* (Address: 1253 4th St. S.W., Washington, D.C. 20024).

Games People Play is of course Eric Berne's famous work (New York: Grove Press, 1964).

"Strategy and Tactics"

NOW's Task Force on the Image of Women (Anne Hall, 149 Dartmouth, Rochester, N.Y.) has material on the National Airlines' and other such actions. The Code of Ethics for domestic work, also mentioned in the chart distinguishing between a bad scene and an issue, was developed by Church Women United. (Write Ms. Carl W. Segerhammer, 4145 Olympiad Dr., Los Angeles, 90043). Household Technicians of America (HTA, c/o NCHE, 1725 K St. N.W., Washington, D.C. 20006) is working from the employees' end, toward organizing domestic labor; according to them, 98 percent are women, 66 percent are black, the average age is 46. HTA works for legislative protections, as well as unionization of domestics.

Women for a Peaceful Christmas (Box 5095, Madison, Wis.), who report "hundreds and hundreds of letters" from their alternative Christmas proposals, are continuing their simpler-lifestyle, peace-oriented activities year round.

Ralph Nader's comment on aging is from *Old Age: The Last Segregation.* It was young women Raiders who worked in nursing homes for "homework" to develop more stringent codes. The material on Project Second Start is from Jolly Robinson (35 West 82nd St., New York, N.Y. 10024), who did her homework. The tax inequity case comparing the lawyer and his secretary was described in *The Spokeswoman* (Vol. 2, No. 5, Nov. 1971). Judith Viorst (3432 Ashley Terrace N.W., Washington, D.C. 20008) and her cohorts worked with Congresswoman Bella Abzug (D-N.Y.) to prepare the bill.

The late Saul Alinsky, through his writing and his Industrial Areas Foundation Training Institute, was the chief proponent of a hard-headed brand of community organizing that is both reviled and revered. Most of the references in this section come from his recent book, *Rules for Radicals* (New York: Random House, 1971). I am indebted to many of his principles, but feel they need reinterpreting and should be applied selectively to be applicable to the organization of women.

The American Association of University Women (AAUW) has a "Blue Book for Analysis and Planning," based upon the organizing questions. It is a guide for discussion, worksheet for charting progress, and a record for evaluating action.

Mother Jones's activities are described in *Appalachian People's History Book* by Suzanne Crowell (Louisville: Southern Conference Educational Fund, 1971). The material on the Action Committee for Decent Childcare is from *The Spokeswoman* (Vol. 2, No. 3, Sept. 1971), and from Heather Booth, ACDC (5006 S. Dorchester, Chicago, Ill. 60615).

"Co-opt the System"

For the human side of the *Abramowicz vs. Lefkowitz* case, read *Abortion Rap* by Diane Schulder and Florynce Kennedy (New York: McGraw-Hill, 1971). For more information on key women's lawsuits see *Women's Rights Law Reporter*. The *Environmental Law Handbook* by Norman J. Landau and Paul D. Rheingold (New York: Ballantine, 1971) describes the legal side of the ecology struggle. *Academic Women, Sex Discrimination and the Law; An Action Handbook* describes resources available to women who experience sex discrimination on campus (MLA Commission on the Status of Women, Wesleyan Station, Middletown, Conn. 06457).

The Atlanta Chapter of NOW, whose experience is desegregating the want ads is reported, may be contacted at P.O. Box 54045, Civic Center Station, Atlanta, Ga. 30308. The chart "Federal Laws Covering Sex Discrimination in Employment" was prepared by B. J. Miller and Ruth McElhinney. For information on the Women's Advocate

Corps of NOW, write Mary Lynn Myers, Rm. 1256, 219 S. Dearborn St., Chicago, Ill. 60604; for *Women's Job Rights,* write Ruth McElhinney, 2648 Stuart St., Berkeley, Ca. 94705.

The Women's Bureau (Department of Labor, Washington, D.C.) has many helpful resource materials now available for women's-rights activists (Write Government Printing Office, Superintendent of Documents, Washington, D.C. 20402). "A Matter of Simple Justice: President's Task Force on Women's Rights and Responsibilities" is one; "Laws on Sex Discrimination in Employment" is another. A "Job Discrimination Handbook, Human Rights for Women" (1129 National Press Bldg., Washington, D.C. 20004) has much factual information. NOW's National Task Force on Compliance and Enforcement (1957 E. 73rd St., Chicago, Ill. 60649) has prepared "Business and Industry Discrimination Kits." All the above are available for small charges.

Help Unsell the War is located at 637 West 125th St., New York, N.Y. 10027. Ad Lib was described by Anne Tolstoi Foster in the *New York Times,* Business and Finance Section (Nov. 22, 1971). The press release form is from *The Organizer's Manual,* an excellent local handbook prepared by Eastside Forum (4840 E. Mercer Way, Mercer Island, Wash. 98040). The address of the KPFA Women's Collective is 2207 Shattuck Ave., Berkeley, Ca. 94704. Nicholas Johnson's *How To Talk Back to Your Television Set* (New York: Bantam, 1970) has good material on how to fight for the fairness doctrine. Also see *How to Protect Citizen Rights in Television and Radio* (Office of Communication, United Church of Christ, 289 Park Ave. South, New York, N.Y. 10010).

Ellen Lurie's *How to Change the Schools* (New York: Vintage, 1970) is full of practical suggestions on how to make your voice heard in school policies.

The Organizer's Manual, prepared by the O. M. Collective (New York: Bantam, 1971), is a handbook of strategy and tactics, geared more to student activism than to women, but with many excellent ideas, such as how to brainstorm. Another such book comes from the civil rights movement: *A Manual for Direct Action,* by Martin Oppenheimer and George Lakey (Chicago: Quadrangle Books, 1965). Both are useful.

Leader of the "Role Your Own" group at Radical Psychiatry was Brian Allen (2333 Webster, Berkeley, Ca.). The Simulation Games are distributed by the Anti-Defamation League of the B'nai Brith (315 Lexington Ave., New York, N.Y.). "Sexism" is produced by Houger & McCaw, Seattle, Wash. It can be ordered through Seattle Chapter of NOW (c/o Carolyn Houger, 600 N.W. 126th Pl., Seattle, Wash. 98107). "Games People Should Play" is available from the Midpeninsula YWCA, 4161 Alma St., Palo Alto, Ca.

The two unlikely arrests in the Palo Alto "riot" were reported in the San Francisco *Chronicle* (July 14, 1970). The night in prison that shocked the judges appeared in the same paper on July 10. "Liferaft Earth" is well described in *The Last Whole Earth Catalog* (Portola Institute, Random House, 1971).

A "movement" catalog for all the media is *Source* (Chicago: Swallow Press, 1971). The address is 1139 S. Wabash Ave., Chicago, Ill. 60605. The slide show on sex tracking in the public schools, and another on media image of women, was prepared by Pat McCormick (Berkeley NOW, P.O. Box 7024, Berkeley, Ca. 94707). For more information on the Committee for Open Media, write Debbie Majteles, 3035 Fulton St., Berkeley, Ca. 94705. KPFA Women's Collective is at 2207 Shattuck Ave., Berkeley, Ca. 94704.

"Money"

Any woman will be encouraged and enlightened by reading about the suffrage struggle. The section on fourteenth-century fund raising is gleaned from Carrie Chapman Catt and Ettie Rogers Shuler, *Woman Suffrage and Politics* (Seattle: Americana Library Paperback, 1970). The authors were activists in the movement.

Daniel Lynn Conrad, the professional fund raiser referred to, teaches classes on the subject in the San Francisco Bay Area (National Action/Study Center, 1805 Pine St., San Francisco, Ca. 94104). "How to Raise Money for NOW" by Jean Powers (207 W. 98th St., Apt. 2C, New York, N.Y. 10025) describes the New York chapter's $1,400 party and many more feminist fund-raising ideas. Also available from NOW: "Feminist Fundraising Is Fun" and "Sister, Can You Spare a Dime?" (1957 E. 73rd St., Chicago, Ill. 60749).

Romula R. Soldevilla's comments were reported in "How to Set the Ground for a Successful Fund Drive," in *Fund Raising Management* (Sept./Oct. 1969). Good material on stockholder action can be found in the pamphlet "Ask for a Woman: Handbook for a Corporate Suffragette" by Marilyn Hall Patel, and published by NOW. The socially conscious mutual funds were reported by columnist Milton Moskowitz, which appeared in the San Francisco *Chronicle* on October 23, 1971. For more information on the subject, write Corporate Information Center, National Council of Churches (475 Riverside Drive, New York, N.Y. 10027).

Part III

Food For All, Inc. is a nonprofit organization funded by the Office of Economic Opportunity (OEO); Grace Olivarez is Executive Director (2875 E. Sky Harbor Blvd., Suite 201, Phoenix, Arizona 85034). Seattle's School for Community Action (c/o YWCA, 1118 5th Ave., Seattle, Wash. 98101) still functions. When last contacted, they were planning a conference on women and justice. Women's Action Alliance has a national office at 200 Park Ave., Rm. 1520, New York, N.Y. It was launched by Gloria Steinem and Brenda Feigen Fasteau.

The Spokeswoman is an independent eight-page monthly newsletter that reports a wide range of women's activities. *Very* useful. Other Movement newsletters include *The Woman Activist* (2310 Balbour Rd., Falls Church, Vt. 22043) and *Women Today* (National Press Building, Washington, D.C. 20004).

Women United is located in the nation's capital (P.O. Box 300, Washington, D.C. 20044). At time of writing the ERA had just passed the Senate, so now the fight moves to state ratification. The coalition may function in new ways.

The Michigan coalition Network for Economic Rights was initiated by women in the United Auto Workers. Olga M. Madar, UAW vice-president, is Chairman pro tem (8000 Jefferson Ave., Detroit, Mich. 48214). NER coalitions are forming in other states, including California, as this is written.

Shirley Chisholm's comments were gleaned from an election rally at Mills College in Oakland. For more on her philosophy, read her autobiography, *Unbought and Unbossed* (Boston: Houghton Mifflin, 1970). The National Women's Political Caucus has headquarters in Suite 707, Warner Building, Washington, D.C. 20004. Local caucuses are now functioning in many states.

The "new shanties on the old plantations" comment is from *The Spokeswoman* (Vol. 2, No. 3, Sept., 1971), which took to task the Institute for Paralegal Training in Philadelphia.

The Calumet Community Congress of Gary, Indiana, given as an example of parallel coalitions, was from a New York Times Service article that appeared in the San Francisco *Chronicle,* Dec. 7, 1970.

Sheila Cahill of Palo Alto is the "conference pro" who kindly put together for me her experience from organizing conferences for the Stanford Alumni Association.

Ruth McElhinney of Women's Jobs Rights edited the manuscript and added a great deal from her own experience. Others who read all or part of it and made many suggestions were Patricia Huckle, Alita Letwin, Ruth Friedlander, and Tanis Walters.